THE eSSeNT TO FLY F

Text by Nick Hart
Images by Henry Gilbey
Diagrams by Nick Hart/Andy Steer

First published in 2006 by Hart Flyshop Ltd
Second edition published in 2009 by Hart Flyshop Ltd

Printed and Designed by Maslands, Tiverton, Devon.

ISBN
0-9553250-1-3
978-0-9553250-1-4

Visit us online at
www.hartflyshop.com

CONTENTS

INTRODUCTION
What is Fly Fishing?

Weighty Issue: There have been many descriptions throughout the years used to sum up what Fly Fishing is really all about. As an introduction we should firstly examine the difference between fly fishing and other forms of angling, namely Coarse and Sea. These sectors of our sport employ mechanical reels (fixed spool or multipliers are widely used) holding large quantities of very thin line known as monofilament. Attached to the end of this line is some kind of weight. This can be a non toxic variety (a legal requirement for coarse anglers) or lead often weighing several ounces, in the case of sea anglers. Other weights come in the form of large baits or possibly metal/plastic lures referred to as spinners, spoons or plugs.

The angler makes a forward stroke with the rod, bringing it to a **controlled, abrupt, stop**. At this point the weight will shoot forward and the very thin line, offering little resistance will have no choice but to follow until gravity takes over, pulling the weight back to earth and resulting in the completed requirement (or skill), a cast. The angler now sits and waits until a fish happens upon the bait or winds/retrieves in steadily (in the case of plugs for example), causing the lure to move in an enticing manner.

Fly Fishing – it's not so different!: So now that we know how other anglers
present their bait to their quarry, what process enables an angler to cast a fly? Well firstly the art of fly casting is actually not so far removed from the methods used to cast when Coarse or Sea Fishing. There are certainly a considerable amount of extra movements required and a necessity for consistent good timing, however, there are similarities and these are discussed below.

Fly Line – The Fly Fishers Weight: Fly Lines are made from a core coated
with PVC plastic and are many times thicker than conventional monofilament fishing line. This provides the necessary weight required to cast. Fly lines vary tremendously as we shall learn later, however, they have one common factor. Each is provided with a number denominating its weight, the scale begins at 0 and rises to 17. The majority of us will only ever use a few of these weights, the most popular choices for Trout fishing in the U.K. being 4, 5, 6, 7 and 8. The numbers were given to each line by an important group known as the Association of Fishing Tackle Manufacturers, or AFTM for short.

AFTM Explained – The AFTM number informs an angler if a line is designed for gentle
presentation of their flies at short distances or long casts using large flies. To simplify this, think of lines as feathers, rocks and boulders. Lines from 0 to 5 are the light lines, the feather. Lines from 6 to 10 are the rocks and finally we have the big guns, the boulders, from 10 to 17. Lines also have a profile (they are rarely of one thickness or diameter throughout) and come in versions designed to float on the surface and sink below. This will be further examined at a later stage.

Putting it all together – So now that we have a weight all we need is a bait or as we
say, a fly. Constructed from fur & feather strapped to a hook, our fly is designed to represent various foods within our quarries diet, this could be an insect of some description, a crustacean or possibly

another small fish, known as a baitfish. This all depends on the species sort, the location and even the time of year or weather conditions. The fly is tied to a long piece of monofilament (referred to as a leader), often in the region of nine to sixteen feet, that has been attached to the end of the fly line. Then using a flexible rod that has been balanced/matched using the AFTM scale, a series of casting strokes are made, finally resulting in a **controlled, abrupt, stop**. Yes, just like Coarse and Sea Fishing! The line shoots off over the water at high speed and the light leader/fly are pulled along with it. Gravity pulls the line and fly to the water at which point the angler begins to retrieve the whole lot back again.

Summing Up – This is very generalised description of fly fishing! There are actually infinite permutations and many years of fun to be enjoyed discovering them, however, to keep things simple always remember that **a cast is formed using the weight of fly line and a controlled, abrupt, stop to deliver it**. The following pages detail the essential tackle and accessories required for successful fly fishing.

Casting with a spin rod. The weight flexing the rod in this instance is the lure in the bottom right hand corner of the image.

Casting with a fly rod. Note the similarity to the picture above. Here the weight of the line is used to 'load' the blank.

KEY POINTS TO REMEMBER

1) Fly lines are available in varying weights.
2) A cast is formed once the rod has come to a Controlled, abrupt, stop.
3) Casting is not difficult

TACKLE

Rods...

Fly Rods

The fly rod is a very important part of our tackle, but, perhaps not so important as our choice of fly line. More of this later. Rods have evolved through the years with materials such as greenheart, bamboo and glass fibre used in their construction. The most popular material on the market nowadays is carbon fibre sheet (rolled into a tubular form referred to as a blank), resulting in incredibly light, yet extremely powerful rods. Rods are made up of a cork handle with a number of rings situated along the blank to carry the line. The rod stores and releases energy (very effectively) when casting. The rod also acts as a shock absorber when playing a fish, protecting the thin leader from sudden lunges, that can result in the monofilament breaking.

Which Rod?

Rods vary in size depending on fish species, size and the constraints of the venue being fished. When fishing enclosed areas such as rivers, a short rod of 6ft to 8ft would be suitable, designed to fish lines from 3 to 5. Such lines are designed for short distances and gentle presentation. If a longer cast is required and the fish encountered are expected to be larger, then a 6 to 8 line may be required, cast using a rod from 9ft to 10ft. This would be the usual choice for anglers fishing on small stillwaters and reservoirs. For very long casts using large flies, when taking on hard fighting species such as Salmon, rods of 10ft through to 15ft could be required. These are generalisations but provide a basic guide to refer to. Later in the booklet the rod will be described in greater detail within the casting section.

KEY POINTS TO REMEMBER

1) Rods are designed to be fished with specific lines designated by the AFTM. Look just above the cork handle to find information regarding the rods line rating written on the blank

2) A rod stores energy that is transferred to the line during a cast.

3) When playing a fish the rod acts as a shock absorber.

4) Think about the venue you will be fishing and the species sort when choosing a suitable rod.

...& Reels

Fly Reels

Fly Reels are used to store the fly line when not in use and are also used to gather it back in at the end of a fishing session or perhaps while playing a fish. Reels have evolved with the times as new materials have become available. Once upon a time reels could weigh pounds and were constructed from brass or even wood. In modern times the use of plastics and lightweight metals such as aluminium has become popular. Reels are made up of a body incorporating a reel foot, this is attached to the rod. Into the body of the reel is fixed a spool holding the fly line, these spools can be interchanged to allow the use of various different fly lines.

Which Reel?

For most U.K. fishing on small stillwaters, reservoirs and rivers a basic reel will suffice providing storage for the line and little more. However, if large powerful species such as Salmon are to be targeted then something a little more advanced maybe required incorporating a disc drag. The drag system is operated using a knob or lever to apply pressure to the spool. This makes it more difficult for a fish to take line, consequently tiring it out quickly or ensuring that it does not run into snags. The spool spins around a centre spindle referred to as the arbour, this can be narrow but in recent times it has become popular to widen the diameter. These reels are called large arbours and allow the line to be stored in nice wide open coils, (more about this in the fly line section) while also allowing line to be retrieved back on to the spool faster than conventional standard arbour models. Cartridge reels allow multiple lines to be stored.

KEY POINTS TO REMEMBER

1) **A reel is designed to store the fly line in neat, open coils.**

2) **Reels are either of a standard arbour or have a large arbour**

3) **Reel selection should be based on the venue and species to be targeted**

4) **Hard fighting species may require a reel equipped with a disc drag**

TACKLE

Fly Lines

Fly Line Facts

As we have previously learnt, the fly line provides the weight required to deliver our fly to the unsuspecting fish. Exactly how this process is achieved appears later on in the casting section. Prior to learning how to cast it is absolutely essential to learn about fly lines and their characteristics.

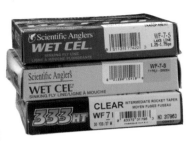

AFTM – Association of Fishing Tackle Manufacturers – Explained

Construction: Fly lines are constructed from a core material such as nylon or braided terylene which is then coated with a PVC or similar plastic material. **It is very important to buy the best line you can afford to ensure this coating is of a high quality.** The line must be as smooth as possible, a characteristic of good quality fly lines. Expect to pay at least £30.00 and above for a good line, but keep in mind that with care it will last several years. To prolong the life of a line ensure that you regularly clean it. Before deciding on a very expensive rod, give the line some thought. **As a rule of thumb, a great line on a not so great rod, is far better than the other way around! Of course a great line supported by a great rod is even better!**

Length: Fly Lines vary from manufacturer to manufacturer but in general the length of a fly line ranges from 27 to 35 yards. A big fish can require a considerable amount more than this, so the fly line is connected to a very low diameter line referred to as **"backing"**. A reasonable quantity of backing is wound on to the reel prior to attaching the fly line. While this assists when playing a large fish it also further expands the diameter of the fly reel, allowing the line to be stored in wide open coils.

Weight: The AFTM number refers to the weight of the line, starting at 0 and rising to 17. **Remember, the higher the number the heavier the line.** This number is not related to the breaking strain of the line in anyway, it merely notifies the angler what rating the line has been given and what style of fishing it will be suitable for. The weights were arrived at using a rather complicated system of American wheat grains, often overlapping and causing confusion. Knowing the weight in grains is in most circumstances, unnecessary, just check the number on the fly line box when purchasing and ensure it matches the rating of your chosen rod.

Profile: This is where things start to become interesting! The fly line has a profile, in other words it varies in thickness along its length. Possibly the most common line in use today is called a **Weight Forward**, or **WF** as categorised by AFTM. Another common line is the **Double Taper** or **DT**. There are many other variations but they are unimportant at this point. The WF is easy to cast with the correct technique and therefore recommended for use by novice to advanced fly anglers. The WF consists of around 10 yards of thick line at the forward section referred to as the **"head"** or

"belly". This tapers prior to the junction between fly line and leader allowing a gradual energy transfer and a delicate presentation of the fly to our fish. After a short rear taper, the majority of the length is taken up by the **"running line"**. This thin line offers very little resistance in the rod rings, the thick belly section pulling it out quickly across the water during casting. It could be argued that this is not so far removed from the process of casting a weight to drag thin monofilament line from the reel as used by coarse and sea anglers.

Density:
Fly lines can be designed to float, sink very slowly or very fast. There are many different lines on the market but as a start the floating fly line will suffice, followed by a slowly sinking line known as an **intermediate** and finally, a medium to fast sinker. Floating fly lines have air bubbles trapped below the outer skin of the line to provide buoyancy. Sinking lines are very thin and manufactured with a dense plastic coating. Sink rates can vary from as little as 1/2 inch per second to 8 inches per second!

The AFTM Code:
If we take all of the above and put it together we can recognise lines as follows. A Weight Forward, number 8 line that floats on the surface would be shortened to **WF8F**, while a Double Taper sinking line with a rating of 10 would appear as **DT10S**.

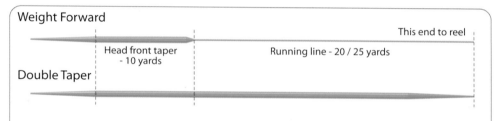

Weight Forward

This end to reel

Head front taper - 10 yards

Running line - 20 / 25 yards

Double Taper

Fly Line Profiles and cross sections

Cross Section of Fly Line showing Core

Cross Section of Floating Fly Line, thick outer skin expanded by air bubbles

Cross Section of Sinking Fly Line, with dense outer skin

KEY POINTS TO REMEMBER

1) **Fly lines have a weight, profile and density.**

2) **A fly line should have a smooth coating.**

3) **Clean fly lines regularly to prolong their life.**

4) **Attach backing to the reel prior to connecting the fly line.**

5) **Fly lines are described using the AFTM system.**

TACKLE

Leaders & Essential Knots

THE FINAL LINK!

Rods, Reels and Lines all need careful selection but so do **Leaders**, after all, other than the hook this is the last link between you, the fly line and your fish! The correct leader is also important to ensure good presentation and accuracy, while a carefully constructed leader system reduces tangles. Remember that the leader is designed to provide an almost invisible link between the fly line and your artificial fly, so always fish the longest leader possible for the given conditions.

Leader Material: Leaders are divided up into nylon, co polymer and fluorocarbon. Use nylon and co polymer for surface fishing and fluorocarbon when going sub surface. The main benefit of fluorocarbon is that it has a low refractory index, in plain English, it doesn't reflect so much light. This results in a leader that is very difficult to see and experiments seem to prove that it is a more effective fish catcher. However, fluorocarbon is prone to sinking and is therefore not a good choice for fishing surface patterns. It is also far more expensive than regular leader material. Ensure you have plenty of spools of leader, consisting of co polymer and fluorocarbon, in varying breaking strains. It is also wise to purchase a substance used to help sink leaders referred to as "mud" or "leader sink". This compound is carefully smeared along the leader to remove any grease and assist the leader to sink below the surface film, extremely important when dry fly fishing. The use of leader sink is only required when fishing with nylon or copolymer, do not use on fluorocarbon.

Knotless Tapered Leaders or KTL are perfect for fishing when accuracy is of paramount importance. Constructed from one piece of extruded nylon, the KTL starts with a very thick **"butt section"** tapering down gradually to a fine tip, sometimes referred to as the "tippet". When the fly line is cast the thick butt section provides a stiff lever action that helps the remaining fine leader to **"turn over"**. The advantage is superb accuracy, excellent strength throughout and a minimum requirement for knots. The disadvantages are that they are expensive, difficult to customise and need to be replaced on a regular basis. KTL are the first choice for most River Trout fishing.

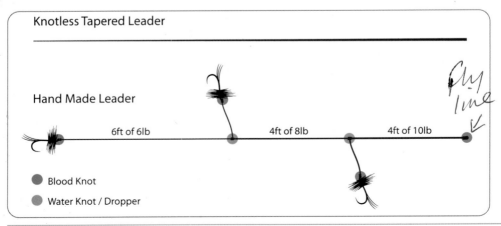

Knotless Tapered Leader

Hand Made Leader

6ft of 6lb   4ft of 8lb   4ft of 10lb

Fly line

● Blood Knot

● Water Knot / Dropper

Hand Made Leaders or **HML** are more economical than the **KTL**, plus they can be customised to suit conditions. As an example a leader of 14ft could be constructed from 4 feet of 10lb line, 4 feet of 8lb line and 6 feet of 6lb line. A **"Water Knot"** is used to join these sections together (see diagram on page 12). Each knot has two **"tag ends"**, one of these remaining arms can be left connected to enable an angler to fish more than one fly, this is called a **"dropper"**. HML are cheap

Always take time when tying knots, they are your last link to the fish!

to construct and several can be made in advance prior to a trip. However, HML are time consuming and do not offer the efficiency of the KTL. HML are ideal for Reservoir fishing.

Braided and Poly Leaders: These often confuse anglers as they are termed leaders. However, think of this type of leader as merely an extension of your fly line. Available in varying densities, they are ideal as a method of sinking flies to a greater depth when used in conjunction with a floating line and regular length of leader. These leaders are only recommended to experienced anglers.

Knots: Every angler must be able to construct knots to attach hooks and connect sections of line. Knots should be carefully formed and pulled together, never jerk the knot suddenly to a close. Ensure that all knots are well lubricated. Think about the hands used to hold the leader and manoeuvre the tag end into position. The "natural" hand should do the work, while the other provides a useful grip to stop everything from unravelling.

KEY POINTS TO REMEMBER

1) **Leaders can be one piece (KTL) or made from varying diameters (HML)**

2) **The leader provides a near invisible link to the fly.**

3) **Gear up with a leader that is strong enough to cope with the size of fish you expect to catch.**

4) **Always lubricate the turns when pulling a knot together.**

5) **As a general rule, Leaders from 4lb to 10lb will provide ample strength to cope with most Trout fishing situations in the U.K.**

6) **In most circumstances leaders should be at least 9ft and above. Don't be afraid to use long leaders, if they are tapered correctly they will work well in conjunction with a good casting technique.**

Fly Fishing Knots

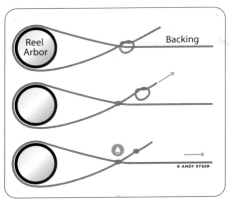

Reel Arbor · Backing

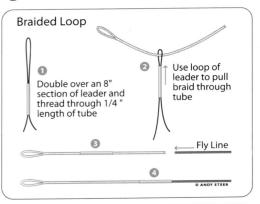

Braided Loop

1. Double over an 8" section of leader and thread through 1/4 " length of tube
2. Use loop of leader to pull braid through tube
3.
Fly Line
4.

© ANDY STEER

Water Knot

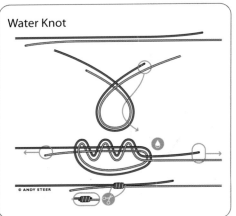

© ANDY STEER

Blood Knot

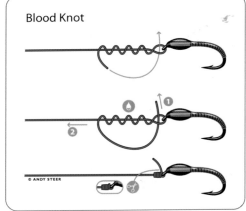

© ANDY STEER

Backing, Fly Line and Leader Connections

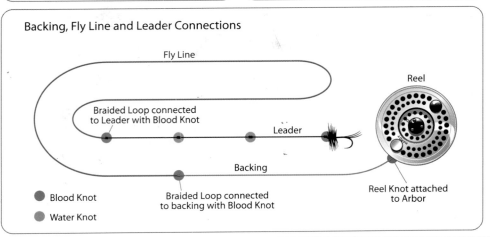

Fly Line

Braided Loop connected to Leader with Blood Knot

Leader

Reel

Backing

Reel Knot attached to Arbor

Braided Loop connected to backing with Blood Knot

● Blood Knot

● Water Knot

Stocking a Fly Box - Wet & Dry Flies

HOW TO GET STARTED

Peering into a well stocked fly box for the first time or making selections from tackle shops can be a daunting experience for the novice. However, the task can be simplified to make the choices far easier allowing anglers to get on with the business of fishing rather than spending most of the session deciding on a fly. Remember that a fly can only catch a fish while in the water!

Dry Flies This group sits on or just in the surface, hence the term "dry". Characteristics include a stiff hackle (see diagram right), sparse body and light wire hook. They imitate flies that have hatched from below the surface or those that have been blown on to the water. Dry Flies can also imitate various beetles and insects such as Ants.

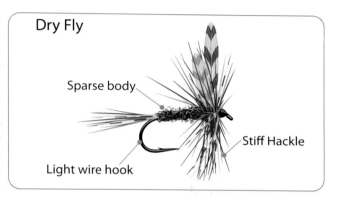

Dry Fly

Sparse body

Light wire hook

Stiff Hackle

Wet Flies This is a large group of fly paterns that are used to fish below the surface. Characteristics include a soft hackle (see diagram below), hairy body, heavy wire hook and even the addition of beads or a lead under body to assist sink rate. Wet flies imitate Nymphs, Larva, Pupa and small fish amongst other things. Most lures (a gaudy selection of feathers designed to arouse aggression within fish) are wet flies.

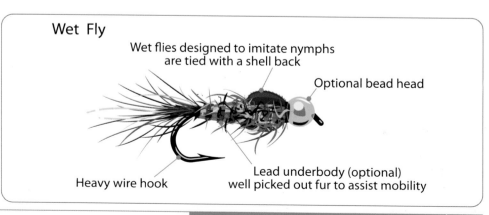

Wet Fly

Wet flies designed to imitate nymphs
are tied with a shell back

Optional bead head

Heavy wire hook

Lead underbody (optional)
well picked out fur to assist mobility

TACKLE

The Essential Selection!

Many anglers struggle to find a range of go anywhere flies that will bring regular success and imitate a wide variety of "fish food" (see page 38) Others struggle to identify which fly to use, when and where. This brief guide lists the essential patterns that every fly angler should be aware of and have stocked within their collection of fur and feather. The following patterns can be used throughout the year and are proven fish catchers. These flies are recommended as absolutely essential in every fly box!Leave home without them, if you dare! The following patterns can be used throughout the year and are proven fish catchers. These flies are recommended as absolutely essential in every fly box!

1.  **Bloodworm:** (Imitates Bloodworm) The larval stage of the chironomid, commonly know to anglers as "Buzzers" (see below). Favours silty lake beds. A food form well worth imitating throughout the year on small stillwaters and reservoirs. Fish on a floating line with a long leader, goldheads will help achieve depth quickly and also stand out amongst the crowd when fish gorge themselves on large quantities of the natural. Sinking lines can be used, especially during cold spells, winter fishing etc., when Trout will be glad to find a Bloodworm or two on offer!

> **Type: Wet Common Features: Curved Body, Long Tail Size: 10 – 14 Colours: Red or Olive Depth: Deep Lines: Floating / Sinking Retrieve: Short Jerky Pulls Fish with It: All Year**

2.  **Buzzer Pupa:** (Imitates Midge Pupa) This fly should spend a lot of time on your leader! The pupae of chironomid midge, starting life as bloodworm (see above) An absolute must in every fly anglers fly box. Buzzers are like "bread & butter" to Trout! Found at a huge range of depths it is possible to fish this fly on every line going, from just below the surface to way down deep. Tactics are many and varied, try under an indicator, fish at range across the wind, great on the washing line or trail behind a small lure in a team of 3 or 4 (see pages 44 - 46 for lake fishing tactics)

> **Type: Wet Common Features: Curved & Segmented Body, Bright Wing Buds Size: 8 – 18 Colours: Black, Red or Olive Depth: All Lines: Floating / Sinking Retrieve: Short Jerky Pulls, Figure 8, Static, Stop & Start Fish with It: All Year**

3.  **Hopper:** (Imitates Adult Midge) The final stage of the chironomid, this pattern represents the adult just as it hatches, legs trailing, struggling to escape from the surface film. Add some floatant such as "Gink" and cast to rising Trout or just leave it to drift on the wind. The secret with this fly is to rarely move it, just wait for a Trout's head to appear. LIFT!

> **Type: Dry Common Features: Strong Hackle, Picked out Body, Trailing Legs Size: 10 – 12 Colours: Black, Claret or Ginger Depth: Surface Lines: Floating Retrieve: Static, Occasionally slow figure 8 Fish with It: All Year**

4.

CDC Bung: (Imitates Adult Midge, Sedge and Terrestrials) Designed

to represent a wide range of food including adult flies and terrestrial insects such as Hawthorns or Beetles. However, this fly is best used not so much as an imitation but as part of a team in conjunction with flies such as Buzzers or Hares Ears. Create a New Zealand Dropper (see page 45) and fish the Bung as an indicator. When a fish takes the subsurface pattern, the Bung will disappear, LIFT! Look out for fish taking this pattern off the surface and try it singularly during a sedge hatch, skittered along the surface.

**Type: Dry Common Features: Large CDC Wing Size: 10 – 12 Colours: Black
Depth: Surface Lines: Floating Retrieve: Static, Steady pulls Fish with It: All Year**

5.

Hares Ear: (Imitates Caddis, various Nymphs and Hoglouse) A great

general pattern for hedged bet fishing. It could be a nymph, perhaps a cased caddis or maybe a hoglouse? Scruffy Hares Ears are best, providing excellent mobility within the fly and the illusion of moving insect legs or perhaps a twitch of a tail. Fish find this hard to resist! Carry weighted and un-weighted versions plus some with Goldheads, there are many and varied patterns available! Fish on its own or in a team of flies, especially on the point when weighted or in the middle dropper position if un-weighted.

**Type: Wet Common Features: Tail, Segmented, Scruffy Body, Shell Back and Thorax
Size: 8 – 14 Colours: Natural / Dyed Olive or Black Depth: Deep / Mid Water
Lines: Floating / Sinking Retrieve: Slow and Fast Figure 8, Steady pulls
Fish with It: All Year**

6.

Damsels Nymphs: (Imitates Damsel Nymphs and small fish)

Trout rarely feed on adult Damsels, a very agile insect that requires a great deal of effort to catch. However, the Nymph is often preyed upon, particularly in summer. The natural has an enticing wiggle when it swims that unfortunately (for it!) attracts the Trouts attention. Artificial patterns should have long to medium length tails and scruffed up bodies to emulate this movement. Just like the Hares Ear, this pattern is available in a wide range of variations.

**Type: Wet Common Features: Long Marabou Tail, Shell Back, Eyes Size: 10 – 12
Colours: Olive / Golden Olive Depth: Deep / Mid Water Lines: Floating / Sinking
Retrieve: Slow and Fast Figure 8, Steady pulls, Fast pulls Fish with It: All Year**

Narrow fly choices down to make the selection process easier.

TACKLE

Stocking a Stillwater Fly Box- The Seasonal Selection!

In addition to the "Essential 6" it is wise to carry a few of the following patterns to copy seasonally available Trout cuisine.

Corixa: (Imitates Lesser Water Boatman) Otherwise known as Lesser Water boatman, the natural regularly turns up in the marrow spoon during autumn. Often found near weed beds, this species has a unique movement that is very attractive to Trout. The paddles are often accentuated in most artificial patterns to provide a good target point. Look around the margins of stillwaters, especially in autumn and during periods of fry activity.

Type: Wet **Common Features: Eyes, Paddles** **Size: 10 – 14** **Colours: White** **Depth: Mid & Shallow Water** **Lines: Floating / Sinking** **Retrieve: Slow and Fast Figure 8, Jerky Pulls, Steady pulls, Fast pulls** **Fish with It: July to September**

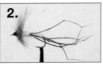

Daddy Long Legs: (Imitates Cranefly) Exactly what it says on the tin, the "Daddy" of all flies! Often found in late summer falling around in the middle of a lake and making quite a commotion. Trout will often drown the fly and then come back to devour it, so be careful not to strike too quickly. This fly will catch all year, even when the naturals are not present and there are all sorts of variations, some even with gold heads! In general, look for a hatch and fish static.

Type: Dry **Common Features: Heavy, stiff hackle, Long knotted legs** **Size: 10 – 12** **Colours: White, Off White, Beige** **Depth: Surface** **Lines: Floating** **Retrieve: Static, Slow Pulls** **Fish with It: Aug to September**

Fry Pattern: (Imitates juvenile fish) Many patterns on the market including Minkies, Zonkers, and Deer Hair Floating Fry. It is possible to imitate the sub surface fry as they are hunted by Trout. Some of the most exhilarating sport is to be had on the surface. Walk along the bank looking for devastating attacks by the fish, as they hunt helpless juvenile coarse fish in a flurry of water spray, lashing tails and biting jaws. Cast a floating fry pattern into the middle of this commotion and simulate the dying fry by occasionally twitching the line.

Type: Wet & Dry **Common Features: Long Tail, Heavy Wing, Clipped Deer Hair Body, Eyes** **Size: 6 – 10** **Colours: White, Grey, Brown or Realistic versions** **Depth: Surface / Mid Water** **Lines: Floating** **Retrieve: Static, Short Jerky Twitch** **Fish with It: Aug to November (and when Fry Activity is observed)**

Lures

Sometimes the fish just won't bite and then a lure can save the day! Modern tactics (see page 45) often use lures as part of a team of flies to attract the Trouts attention. Once the feeding instinct has been aroused, Trout regularly turn on the other patterns in the team, such as Buzzers or Hares Ears. Black Lures are proven fish takers in a wide range of circumstances.

1. **Cormorant:** Great general attractor that could even be taken for a buzzer in small sizes. Cormorants incorporate a number of important features including a highly mobile wing and iridescent peacock herl body. Available in many variations and a pattern that can be fished throughout the year with confidence.

> **Type: Wet Size: 8 – 14 Colours: Black Depth: All Lines: Floating / Sinking Retrieve: All Fish with It: All Year**

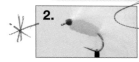

2. **Cats Whisker:** The Cats Whisker has to be one of the most popular still water Trout Fishing Lures. The standard fly sports a white wing over a fluorescent yellow body, although many variations are available that incorporate flash and other eye catching triggers. The mobile wing and contrasting colours fool many Trout, especially stock fish that have been newly introduced to a venue.

> **Type: Wet Size: 8 – 14 Colours: White/Fluorescent Yellow or Green Depth: All Lines: Floating / Sinking Retrieve: All Fish with It: All Year**

3. **Booby:** Err Hum! So called for obvious reasons, the Booby has an ample buoyant cleavage that many Trout find hard to resist! For years used on very fast sinking lines, popped up off the lake bed. This tactic works well but in recent years the "Washing Line" (see page 46) has taken over as a highly successful technique. Stock up with varied eyes for more or less buoyancy. A long leader, fished with a floating line, Booby on the point and Buzzers on the droppers can be devastatingly effective. Do not use when catch & releasing.

> **Type: Wet Size: 10 – 14 Colours: Many and varied! Coral, Peach, Orange, White and Black are favourites Depth: All Lines: Floating / Sinking Retrieve: Static, Slow Figure 8 Fish with It: All Year**

(Right) A well stocked fly box can be a daunting prospect, especially for novice anglers. However, with a good stock of buzzer imitations, a few hares ear nymphs, damsels and lures, most situations are catered for. Remember that very often the depth and speed of retrieve is far more important than the actual fly itself! Crazy, but TRUE!!!

TACKLE

Stocking a River Fly Box- The Essential Six!

When lake fishing, the depth and speed of retrieve is critical, often the fly becomes secondary. Conversely the river angler is rarely retrieving the line to impart life, this is achieved through the natural current. The quarry is often wild and suspicious, which requires the angler to observe the natural environment, choosing flies accordingly. Casts must be accurate and well presented. These six essential flies provide a good general foundation to any river anglers fly box and can be used in confidence regularly throughout the season, carry them in a wide range of size and shade.

River Wet Flies

Czech Nymph: (Imitates Caddis Larvae) A very heavy pattern designed to achieve depth quickly, especially in fast flowing water. Many shades available and a proven catcher of fish feeding on Caddis Larvae, even though it is termed a nymph! Use it in a team of flies to pull small, lightweight patterns down close to the river bed.

Size: 8 – 16 Colours: Natural Hares Ear, Olive, Black Water Condition: Fast / Medium Depth: Deep

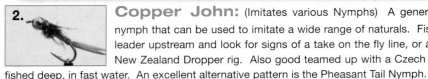

Copper John: (Imitates various Nymphs) A general all round nymph that can be used to imitate a wide range of naturals. Fish on a long leader upstream and look for signs of a take on the fly line, or add below a New Zealand Dropper rig. Also good teamed up with a Czech Nymph and fished deep, in fast water. An excellent alternative pattern is the Pheasant Tail Nymph.

Size: 12 – 18 Colours: Copper, Olive, Black Water Condition: Fast / Medium / Slow Depth: Deep / Mid Water

Spiders: (Imitates - Small drowning Stoneflies) Traditional patterns such as the Snipe & Purple or Partridge & Orange are fished down stream in shallow, fast flowing water. Some techniques also adopt an upstream style. The fly is not designed to represent a spider, but in fact drowning flies that have had trouble hatching. Very good during Stonefly hatches of species such as the Needle or Willow Fly

Size: 14 – 16 Colours: Black, Purple, Orange, Silver Water Condition: Fast / Medium Depth: Shallow

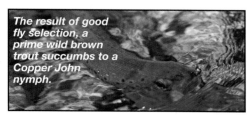
The result of good fly selection, a prime wild brown trout succumbs to a Copper John nymph.

River Dry Flies

1.

Parachute Adams: (Imitates - Mayfly, Various Up Wings) Traditionally dry flies came equipped with "split wings", carefully created from feather fibre and incorporated into many famous fly patterns. These have been superseded in modern day fly angling by a generation of flies known as "parachutes", which are not only simple to tie but also less likely to twist a fine leader. Parachute flies sit down in the water, looking just as if a natural is about to hatch or perhaps floating helpless upon the current. The Adams is a great general pattern that can be used in large sizes to imitate Mayflies and in small sizes to imitate a wide range of other "Up Wings" (see page 41) Carry in varied body colourations, try as an indicator fly when fishing New Zealand style (see page 51)

Size: 10 – 20 Colours: Grey, Olive, Black Water Condition: Fast / Medium / Slow

2.

F Fly: (Imitates - Hatching Midge, Some Up Wings, Ants, Small Beetles) This is an outstanding little fly, so simple and yet so effective! Referred to as an "Emerger"; a hatching fly, half in and half out of the surface film. Particularly good when tiny midge are hatching, resulting in gentle "sips" from the fish as they sit nonchalantly feeding upon their helpless victims. However, body colours can be varied to imitate a wide range of natural insects, a Black F Fly is a great Ant pattern for example, or tie it with an Olive body to imitate a Blue Winged Olive (BWO). When fishing streamy water, look for areas of calm where flies often become trapped and flick a gentle cast to the point where calm and fast water meet. This section of river is often referred to as a seam.

Size: 12 – 20 Colours: Black, Dark & Medium Olive, Claret Water Condition: Medium / Slow

3.

Elk Hair: Caddis/Sedge (Imitates Adult Caddis/Sedge) Caddis flies (also referred to as Sedge), are a large species providing a reasonable meal for hungry Trout and Grayling. However, the adult flies can be tough to catch as they skitter around on the surface or deposit their eggs. Very often the fish will turn their attention to the Caddis Larvae or Pupa, in which case a Czech Nymph is a wise choice of fly. Fish the Elk Hair with confidence in fast streamy water and don't be afraid to twitch this pattern a little by retrieving the fly line if fishing a natural drift provides no success. Also an excellent indicator for New Zealand style.

Size: 10 – 20 Colours: Grey, Olive, Black Water Condition: Fast / Medium Depth: Fast / Medium

CASTING

Getting Started
Casting - Fly Fishing Glue!

The ability to cast accurately and with delicate presentation is a fundamental skill that every fly angler should possess. Casting is in fact the glue that holds the entire process of fly fishing together. No matter how far an anglers knowledge may extend regarding the quarries habitat, diet and characteristics, this information becomes redundant without the necessary skills required to make a delicate presentation of the artificial. Novice anglers should initially learn the Roll Cast (Page 23) in order to maintain safety at all times and straighten the line, although this is also a useful cast in enclosed circumstances such as rivers.

Next on the list is the Overhead Cast (Page 26), perhaps the most frequently used skill and an ideal method of achieving distance. Casting involves "mind & muscle" co ordination that will be much more receptive to practice enjoyed on a "little and often basis". When practicing pay particular attention to form of each casting stroke, maintain a relaxed arm and work on making everything as smooth as possible. One particular mistake is to launch into another cast, just after a bad one, particularly when frustrated. Instead, use a smooth roll cast to straighten the line, ensure the tip of the rod is low to the water and then begin.

Try to allow several seconds between each practice cast because when actually fishing, there will certainly be a time elapse between each cast. Learning in this way provides some kind of reality and trains the all important mind and muscle coordination into a routine that should make for a consistent casting stroke over time. This approach should be adopted for all casting including the Double Haul (Page 32) in particular which is an advanced cast required for long distances, casting into the wind and accuracy.

Fly Casting ... Complicated? Many anglers feel that fly casting is complicated, this is NOT so! Casting is as simple as learning how to generate speed within the fly rod which is then transferred to the line. An element of timing will be required and of course a great deal of practice. Learning how to drive a car takes several sessions to become proficient, fly casting is similar, but soon the movements become second nature just the same as shifting gear.

Hand Position: To facilitate casting try to ensure minimal movement, especially of the wrist, while ensuring that the casting arm remains relaxed. Pay attention to where your hand stops on both forward and back casts. The thumb is a useful device to assist in ensuring high back casts, correct positioning on the forward cast and to assist in beating the dreaded "wrist break" so often the downfall of many fly fishers.

Clock Face: Observing hand positions is one tried and tested method of learning where to position the rod while casting, another is to imagine each position in relation to the hands upon a clock. The diagram on page 26 demonstrates this method. Finally, prior to explaining the various casts required to get started in fly fishing, always remember that there is no substitute for tuition provided by a qualified casting instructor. Look for recognised casting certificates such as AAPGAI when choosing an instructor and preferably opt for instruction provided by a coach who provides courses/tuition on a frequent basis.

CASTING

GRIP

There are definite ways to hold a fly rod and conversely, incorrect methods! Firstly regard the grip not as a white knuckled squeeze causing the arm to shake and the muscles in your wrist to tense, but consider allowing the rod to merely sit within your palm. Just as if you were offering someone a friendly handshake. In fact refer to the physical act of supporting the fly rod as merely a "hold", make this as relaxed as possible and your fly casting technique will certainly see the benefit.

Thumb on top: When "holding" the fly rod it is wise to place your thumb on the top of the handle with the fingers wrapped gently around the cork. This method provides a powerful support and also allows for excellent accuracy. Most people prefer to situate their thumb up near the section of handle joining with the blank, with a reel attached this makes for a superb balance point and also provides good leverage when casting. However, it is not incorrect for an angler to place their hand further down the handle, close to the reel. The main consideration is that the "grip/hold" is comfortable to the individual.

First finger top: Some anglers place their first finger on top of the cork handle. This style is superb for use with small river rods sporting slim handles. However, the thumb on top method is just as good and far better when long casting is required. One other use for the finger on top grip is for those anglers finding difficulty in controlling their wrist when casting. It is impossible (short of breaking it!) to bend a first finger back beyond the top of the hand, assisting newcomers to fly fishing when attempting to make a high back cast.

BEWARE!

Incorrect Grip/Hold: Grabbing hold of the rod is not recommended. This method does not allow for good support while casting.

STANCE

How we stand while fishing/casting is an important consideration, especially when learning advanced casts such as the "Speys". However, within reason, so long as the stance is comfortable to the individual and the physics of making a cast are adhered to, there is certainly allowance for a variety of foot positions. Stances are referred to as "closed" and "open".

Closed Stance: This is a traditional way of standing, common place when river fishing and excellent for accuracy. Right handed casters would place their right foot forward, toe pointing at the target, with their left foot pointing in the same direction but ever so slightly behind the lead foot. The opposite foot would be placed forward for left hand casters.

Open Stance: A much more modern stance, perhaps a little more comfortable than the closed stance and superb when distance casting with techniques such as double hauling. If right handed, place the left foot forward, with the toe pointing at a 90 degree angle away from the target. Place the right foot in a similar position around 1' to 2' behind the leading foot. Again for left handed casting reverse this positioning.

LINE ANCHOR

Good Anchor: When casting the line must remain tight at all times throughout the rod. This will cause the line to flex the blank that will in turn transfer speed back into the line and create a cast. A good anchor is created with the non casting hand (left hand for a right handed caster and vice versa), notice the line is straight.

Bad Anchor: In this photograph a poor anchor is demonstrated with the line hanging loose, this will result in slack during the cast and a far from perfect result. The rod is also pointing skywards, this is incorrect, always start each cast with the rod tip low to the water surface.

CASTING

Getting Started Casting
The Roll Cast Explained

Cast 1 – The Roll Cast

It is very important when attempting an overhead cast to ensure that the line is straight beforehand. There are a number of reasons for this, but the primary consideration is "SAFETY". Casting with a slack line will cause the line to suddenly catapult towards the angler resulting in possible injury. Although accidents are rare, it should be noted that a hat and eye protection are mandatory equipment to ensure no damage is sustained to the eyes or head.

The Roll Cast has many uses, including casting in enclosed conditions, fishing the fly to the shoreline and surfacing a sunken line prior to casting, however, for the novice it is the perfect cast to learn to ensure that the line is straight when performing overhead casts or similar. Here's how …

Step by Step – The Roll Cast.

1) With a closed stance (see page 22) begin with the rod tip placed close to the waters surface.

2) Using the elbow, NOT the wrist, elevate the rod tip to the 10 o' clock position.

3) Tilt the thumb/rod slightly away from the body and draw the rod back until the thumb is reasonably upright and situated at around eye level.

4) At this point glance behind to ensure that a "D Loop" has been formed. There should be a length of line remaining in the water.

5) To complete the cast make a gradually accelerated forward movement, coming to an abrupt yet controlled stop, aiming the rod tip at around 10 o'clock and in exactly the same direction as the line remaining in the water. As the line straightens in mid air, smoothly follow through allowing the line to present gently upon the waters surface, the cast completed with the rod returning once again to a position just above the waters surface.

The Roll Cast – How it Works.

1) The "D Loop" (imperative for good roll casting technique) is weight hanging below the rod tip.

2) As the forward cast is made this weight attempts to break the drag (or "stick") created by the line remaining in the water.

3) As it does so the line places tension upon the rod tip, flexing or "loading" it.

4) The rod comes to a stop and the energy now stored in the rod transfers to the line, creating a "loop" and sending the line off across the waters surface. Simple, but VERY effective!

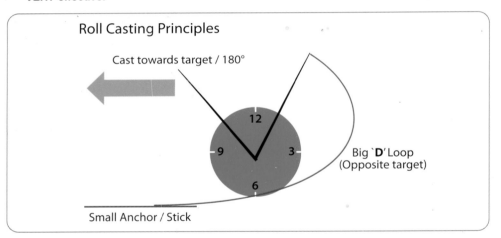

Roll Casting Principles

Cast towards target / 180°

12

9   3

Big 'D' Loop
(Opposite target)

6

Small Anchor / Stick

TOP ROLL CASTING TIPS

1) Ensure a large "D Loop" is formed.

2) Ensure a short section of fly line remains in the water.

3) Always cast in the same direction as the "D Loop" and line remaining in the water.

4) This can be summed up as "Big D, Small Stick and 180 Degrees". Remembering these points will lead to favourable results in most circumstances.

Roll Cast Image Sequence

1. Start Low

2. Lift using elbow to 10 o'clock

3. Angle rod slightly away from body and draw thumb back to upright position. Check for 'D'!

4. Accelerate... (think of hammer tap or swat the fly!)

5. Controlled stop. Aiming rod at 10 o'clock position.

6. Allow line to extend.

Fault Finding - Roll Cast

No 'D' loop, broken wrist!

1.

Stopping too low!

2.

Crossing over!

3.

CASTING

The Overhead Cast Explained

Cast 2 - Overhead Cast

Once the Roll Cast has been practiced it is possible to move on to perhaps the most common of fly fishing casts, the Overhead. This cast allows for very high line speeds and minimal disturbance in the water. Perhaps the main benefit of overhead casting is the ability to obtain long distance presentations, impossible with a standard Roll Cast as the tension of the line becomes stronger with increased distance. Eventually the "D Loop" is no longer large/heavy enough to counteract the drag of the line in the water and the Roll Cast will fail. The answer is to remove the drag effect by placing the line in the air for a period of time, otherwise known as Overhead Cast. Following is a simple explanation of how to perform an Overhead Cast. Always remember to start with a straight line. Hat and eye protection are mandatory to ensure no damage is sustained to the eyes or head.

Step by Step – The Overhead Cast.

1) With a closed stance (see page 22) begin with the rod tip placed close to the waters surface.

2) Using the elbow, NOT the wrist, elevate the rod tip to the 10 o' clock position. Note that this is exactly how the Roll Cast begins. Ensure that the line is "peeled" from the water steadily, a little faster than when performing a roll cast. Do not pause at 10 o' clock as this will allow the line to fall slack, instead ...

3) As soon as the rod arrives at 10 o' clock accelerate swiftly (but smoothly!) so that the thumb halts in line with the eye, stopping in the peripheral vision around 6 to 12 inches away. Once again, check the thumbnail, it should be almost vertical to ensure a high back cast and firm wrist, do not allow the wrist to pivot or "break". The rod should stop at around 1 o' clock, however, pay more attention to the hand and thumb position.

4) It is now important to pause, allowing the fly line to straighten and begin loading the rod. Timing methods to assist include "tick – tock" said out loud during the cast. The "tick" allows the line to straighten and the "tock" sends it forward. Alternatively based on your instructors advice it may be worthwhile trying

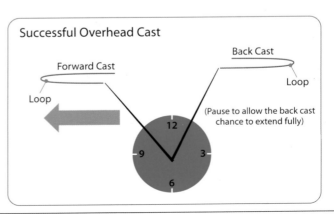

Successful Overhead Cast

Back Cast

Forward Cast

Loop

Loop

(Pause to allow the back cast chance to extend fully)

12

9   3

6

"wait – push" or "1,2 – 3,4" Experiment with timing as some individuals have a fast paced casting style while others are much slower. In a very short while, with practice, it will be unnecessary to chant.

5) To complete the cast make a gradually accelerated forward movement, coming to an abrupt yet controlled stop, aiming the rod tip at around 10 o'clock. As the line straightens in mid air, gradually follow through allowing the line to present gently upon the waters surface, the cast completed with the rod returning once again to a position just above the waters surface. Again, it should be noted that the cast finishes in a similar manner to the Roll Cast. In fact, when casting always use elements of other casts where possible to assist the learning process while also creating a consistent foundation of casting skills. The key to all casting is to practice regularly for short periods of time.

The Overhead Cast – How it Works.

1) The rod begins loading smoothly as the line is "peeled" from the waters surface.

2) When the rod halts on the back cast a "loop" is formed and the line is allowed to straighten out.

3) The straight line flexes/loads the rod so that when the rod stops the energy stored in the rod transfers to the line.

4) Another loop is formed and the line opens out above the water, before gravity takes over and pulls it back down. Once again, simple, but VERY effective!

False Casting & Shooting Line

"False Casting" is the term applied to Overhead Casting when the line is allowed to remain in mid air for 2/3 strokes. An experienced caster can then carefully release controlled amounts of line with each new forward cast, releasing just after "tock, push or 3,4" This process adds additional weight to the rod, creating more bend in the blank and resulting in higher line speeds. False casting allows for minimal water disturbance and maximum distance.

Good Hand Position demonstrating a controlled wrist which will result in a high back cast. Note the link between eye and thumb.

What is a Casting Loop?

Casting is all about forming "loops", a phrase used to describe the shape of line as it leaves the rod tip on the back and forward stroke of an overhead cast. A loop is also formed as the rod stops on the forward stroke of a roll cast, during double hauling and all other casting techniques. Loops can be good, described as "tight" or "narrow" or bad, described as "large" or "wide".

Tight loops are aerodynamic and exactly what an angler is looking for. Tight loops cut through the air quickly, having little air resistance and assist high lines speeds, accuracy and distance. To create a tight loop, ensure that the rod is stopped in the correct position during forward and backward casts.

Conversely wide loops are a cardinal casting sin! The most likely cause is lack of line speed and stopping the rod in an incorrect position. This action pulls the line open, resulting in a loop with a large air resistance. This will cause the line to slow down resulting in poor turnover and presentation. Casts made with a wide loop are more likely to be splashy and achieve less distance.

How is a Loop Formed?

A loop is formed during the casting stroke. As the rod loads under the weight of line, it pulls it forward through the air. At the point when the rod stops, energy from the blank is delivered into the fly line sending it off at speed and creating a loop in the process. Beware, it is very important to have an anchor point, provided by the line controlling hand, without this a loop cannot be formed as the line will no longer be under tension. (See page 22)

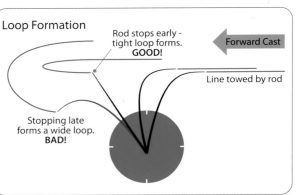

Loop Formation

Rod stops early - tight loop forms. GOOD!

Forward Cast

Line towed by rod

Stopping late forms a wide loop. BAD!

TOP OVERHEAD CASTING TIPS

1) **Roll Cast to straighten the line. Use the elbow to begin the cast and "peel" the line steadily. Do not stop the stroke after the initial lift!**

2) **Watch the wrist and try to stop the thumbnail reasonably upright on the back cast.**

3) **Pause for the back and forward casts using something to remember the timing, "tick – tock" for example.**

4) **Only release (shoot) line once the rod has come to a complete halt on the forward cast**

Overhead Cast Image Sequence

1. Start Low

2. Peel line gently to 10 o'clock using elbow

3. Accelerate (thumb level with eye)

4. Pause, allow line to extend

5. Rod loads, accelerate to ...

6. ... a controlled, abrupt, stop

7. Allow line to extend above the water ...

8. ... and return to the start position

Fault Finding - **Overhead Cast**

Slack line!

1.

Aggressive lift off!

2.

Broken wrist! Low back cast!

3.

Uneven application of power leading to the dreaded tailing loop!

4.

Stopping too low!

5.

This is what it's all about! Launching a tight loop to an unsuspecting fish.

CASTING

Fly Casting Analogies & Principles

Good Roll Casts

1) Big D, Small Line Stick & 180 degrees.

2) When applying the power, think of swatting a fly with a newspaper or tapping a nail into a wall.

3) Stop the rod as if your hand had connected with a wall and can no longer travel forwards.

Bad Roll Casts

1) Pierre slurping his soup, a sign that there is too much line stuck in the water.

2) Spaghetti Bolognese, the result if far too much power is applied, too little or the rod tip is forced towards the water.

Good Overhead Casts

1) When making a back cast think of flicking paint from the rod tip

2) Imagine painting a ceiling to stop the rod rotating in the hand and to ensure a straight rod path

3) When applying power to the forward cast, imagine a very gentle tap with a hammer or better still, the hand suddenly coming into contact with a wall.

4) Timing can be assisted by saying "tick – tock"

5) Think, "Less is More", allow the rod and line to do the majority of the work.

Bad Overhead Casts

1) Many people are heard to say that casting a fly is like cracking a whip. This is NOT so! If the casts sounds like a whip being cracked, slow the timing down and allow the back cast to extend fully.

2) Dead Rod. If the rod feels lifeless, add a little speed to the back cast, think about the timing and ensure that when shooting line that it is only released when the rod has come to a complete halt.

3) Spaghetti Bolognese, the result if far too much or too little power is applied, timing is poor or the rod tip is forced towards the water.

The Double Haul Explained

Double hauling is in fact a technique, rather than a cast in its own right, involving carefully choreographed pulls on the fly line using the line or anchor hand while the casting stroke is in motion. This process creates great tension on the line, forming a deep bend within the blank which transforms into increased line speed as the rod unloads. The ability to create extra speed within the rod is highly desirable as the end result is longer and more accurate casting. However, hauling on the back cast or forward cast (a single haul), or both (double haul), should only be attempted once a sound foundation of casting knowledge has been achieved, practiced until the technique is consistent. As always, head and eye protection are mandatory to ensure no damage is sustained to the eyes or head and casting tuition is recommended with a qualified AAPGAI instructor.

Step by Step – Double Hauling

1) An open stance is recommended (see page 22), begin with the rod tip placed close to the waters surface and both hands close together.

2) Using the elbow, NOT the wrist, elevate the rod tip to the 10 o' clock position. Note that this is exactly how the Roll Cast and Overhead Cast begins. Ensure that the line is "peeled" from the water steadily, do not pause at 10 o' clock as this will allow the line to fall slack, instead, as soon as the rod arrives at 10 o' clock accelerate swiftly (but smoothly!) so that the thumb halts in line with the eye, stopping in the peripheral vision around 6 to 12 inches away. At the same time pull downwards with the line controlling hand, a short, swift pull, rather like bouncing a ball on the ground and say "HAUL!"

3) Once again, check the thumbnail, it should be almost vertical to ensure a high back cast and firm wrist, do not allow the wrist to pivot or "break". It is now important to pause, allowing the fly line to straighten and begin loading the rod. As the line stretches out behind, follow with the line controlling hand while reciting "FEED!", until it is positioned once more, together with the rod hand. This will enable the start of the second hauling motion.

4) The second haul comes throughout the forward stroke, ensure that the haul is short and made downwards, towards the ground and repeat "HAUL!" once more. This is once again a swift pull, rather like bouncing a ball.

5) With the haul complete the rod should now be positioned in the 10 o'clock / 11 o'clock area.

6) Release the line while finishing with "FEED!", and gradually follow through, allowing the line to straighten fully in mid air before arriving once again at the start position.

> **NOTE:** It is advised to practice the movements of the double haul in slow motion, while over grass or similar. Practice stage 2 and 3 first and then 4 and 5. As the technique improves, speed everything up until eventually the line is in mid air and both hands are coordinated.

The Double Haul – How it Works.

1) The rod begins loading smoothly as the line is "peeled" from the waters surface. The line is pulled with the line controlling hand, creating an even greater load on the rod.

2) The rod unloads into the back cast, resulting in a very high line speed, meanwhile the line controlling hand gives the rod back some line, increasing the weight and load upon the blank once the line pulls tight.

3) The deep bend now formed within the blank is improved even more as the hand once again pulls on the line, creating yet more tension and line speed.

4) Another loop is formed, moving at high speed as the line opens out above the water, before gravity takes over and pulls it back down.

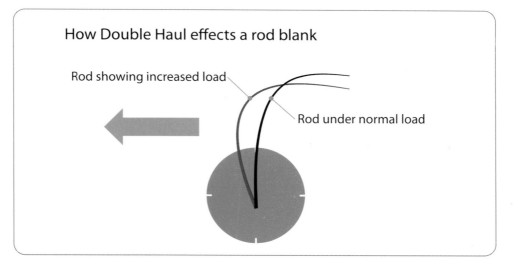

How Double Haul effects a rod blank

Rod showing increased load

Rod under normal load

TOP DOUBLE HAULING TIPS

1) **Build each step up slowly while casting over grass. Coordinate the hands for the back cast and then the forward cast. As the technique improves, begin accelerating the process.**

2) **Ensure that hauls are short and that the line is pulled down, not out to the side.**

3) **Use Haul and Feed to assist with the timing of each cast, keeping all hauls and casting strokes as smooth as possible.**

4) **Use an open stance when double hauling.**

Double Haul Image Sequence

1. Start Low

2. Pull down on line, chant 'HAUL'

3. Bring hands together, chant 'FEED'

4. Pull down on line, chant 'HAUL'

5. Let go of line, chant 'FEED'....

6. ... and follow line to water

Fault Finding - **Double Haul**

1. Long outward haul. BAD!

1.

2. Slack Line. BAD!

2.

10 TOP FLY CASTING TIPS

1) Ensure tackle is balanced using the AFTM scale, see page 8.

2) Novice anglers should only cast during reasonable weather conditions in the first instance. Do not cast in high winds until experienced. Never cast without head and eye protection.

3) Start all casting sessions with a Roll Cast and ensure a straight line.

4) Beware of breaking the wrist.

5) Pay attention to hand/arm movements and positioning at all times, do not look straight out across the water! The clock system is another guide to assist with rod positioning.

6) Always maintain a straight line/rod path. Think of archery arrows or darts, we do not attempt to fire these objects around corners as accuracy and power would be greatly reduced.

7) Think of everyday actions when casting to assist learning the movements required. For example, when applying power to the roll cast remember how to "swat a fly" Approach carefully, build up the acceleration and finish with a controlled flick or tap. When overhead casting think about "flicking paint" from the rod on the back cast to create adequate line speed. To maintain a straight line path, think of painting the ceiling. All casting should be smooth.

8) Most casts end with a controlled, abrupt stop.

9) Allow the rod and line to do the work. Think "less is more" rather than using unnecessary amounts of power to try and achieve distance for example. Casting is all about technique, allowing the rod to place speed within the line. Brute force does not work!

10) Practice on a regular basis (over water where possible) and go for short sessions. "Little & Often" will assist consistency and ability far better than exhaustive practice sessions.

TROUT ANATOMY

Trout Senses

With the equipment packed, fly box stocked and casting honed the next step is to put the whole lot together and go fishing! But, before arriving at the waters edge it is very important to investigate the anatomy as well as the feeding habits of the species pursued, without this fundamental knowledge all those carefully tied flies and tight loops will go to waste!

Hearing: There are many theories surrounding how Trout (fish) hear and it is common for anglers to suddenly break into a whisper when approaching an unsuspecting target, but a loud conversation will not ruin a chance, heavy foot falls will be the culprit. Trout alongside many other fish species possess an incredibly sensitive area running down each side, referred to as a lateral line which is designed to pick up vibrations that assist the fish in finding prey and avoiding obstacles. The lateral line will also register clumsy wading!

Smell: Fish are able to pick up scents. Some scientists believe that this is how a Salmon returns to the same river it first inhabited as a juvenile fish prior to spawning. When Trout fishing ensure that no strong odours touch fly or leader, especially substances such as sun block or tobacco.

Other Requirements and Features of a Trouts Anatomy:

Trout need highly oxygenated water to exist. Reservoir Trout will swim vast distances to maintain the flow of water over their gills, often cruising just subsurface and most often positioned in the direction of an oncoming wind. Lake anglers should use this information to find likely holding areas such as feeder streams while River anglers should be observant of rapids, riffles and similar areas of disturbed water high in oxygen. When a Trout is finally hooked remember that their body is pure muscle propelled by a tail designed for high speed travel away from danger and to intercept prey. Once hooked a fish will display these characteristics in the form of strong runs and aerobatic displays designed to shed the hook, so be ready to give the fish line and keep the rod high. Above all be observant of any likely snags that could provide refuge for a confused Trout, wild fish in particular know their habitat intimately and will make use of every available opportunity.

Highly oxygenated water, perfect trout habitat!

Anatomy of a Trout

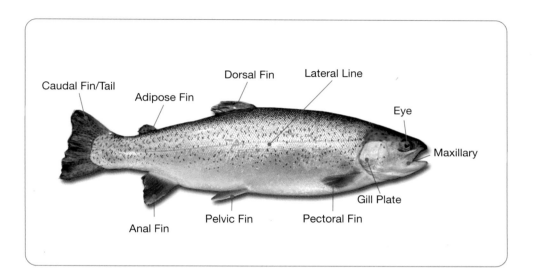

Caudal Fin/Tail
Adipose Fin
Dorsal Fin
Lateral Line
Eye
Maxillary
Gill Plate
Pectoral Fin
Pelvic Fin
Anal Fin

A Trouts-Eye View

Vision: Trout boast extremely good vision when looking forwards and to the side, there is also strong evidence to support the fact that they see in colour. When approaching the quarry an angler must try not to cast shadows or make sudden movements that could alert the Trout to their presence and pay particular attention to leader construction. Tapering a leader (see page 10) improves turnover

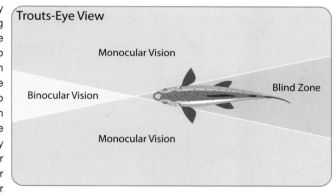

Trouts-Eye View

Monocular Vision
Binocular Vision
Blind Zone
Monocular Vision

assisting the correct presentation of an artificial. Ensure that this last link to angler, fly and fish is as inconspicuous as possible. River anglers often approach fish from behind to take advantage of their blind zone, see diagram right Always remember that Trout look upwards for their food, so if the artificial is below the fishes holding station it will not be seen! When choosing an artificial pay attention to size and colour as Trout, especially wild Trout, can become incredibly selective ignoring inadequate presentations with annoying regularity while feasting upon naturals with gay abandon. Select the correct pattern and the tide will turn!

FISH FOOD # Entomology

The word entomology strikes terror into the hearts of many fly anglers! But, try not to become caught up in long Latin names and worrying if your nymph imitation has enough tails, instead, look at the basic facts. Fish have very little intelligence and rely heavily on instinct, therefore a fly that arouses such instinct, presented carefully and coupled with a logical approach to tactics is likely to succeed. The following diagram shows a variety of common fish food.

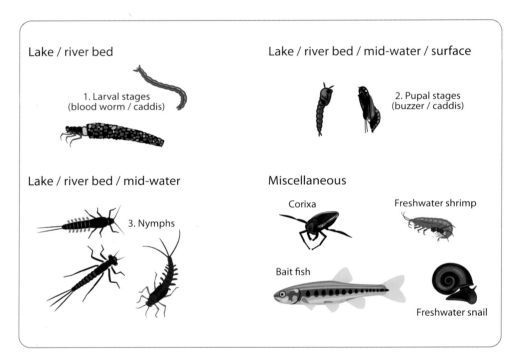

Lake / river bed

1. Larval stages
(blood worm / caddis)

Lake / river bed / mid-water / surface

2. Pupal stages
(buzzer / caddis)

Lake / river bed / mid-water

3. Nymphs

Miscellaneous

Corixa

Freshwater shrimp

Bait fish

Freshwater snail

The Four Orders of Flies

Observation when fishing is essential. Spot a natural insect, find a likely imitation and then make a gentle presentation to the quarry; this is fly fishing summed up in a sentence more or less! However, to fully understand what artificial fly to use, when and where, a working knowledge of the natural insects available and their lifecycle is required. Check under rocks in rivers or look at the edge of a lake to find all sorts of clues. Another method, particularly relevant for river anglers is knowledge regarding "The Four Orders of Flies". Each fly can be identified as a Flat Wing, Up Wing, Roof Wing, or Hard Wing. Catch a fly (look on the water surface, around trees, bushes etc.,) and place on the palm of the hand; as the natural insect rests observe the appearance of the wing and the direction in which it is pointing. The diagram featured will assist with identification.

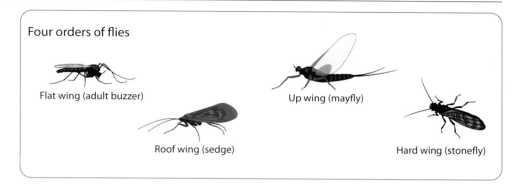

Four orders of flies

Flat wing (adult buzzer)

Up wing (mayfly)

Roof wing (sedge)

Hard wing (stonefly)

Flat Wing Flies (e.g. Midge / Cranefly)

Flat wing flies are consumed on a regular basis by Trout and in some circumstances this group of flies may total three quarters of the overall diet. Present throughout the year, this species can be relied upon to generate a feeding response in many conditions but especially during the spring and summer months. The diagram on page 40 details the lifecycle and see Stocking a Stillwater Fly Box on page 14 for the essential artificial flies required to imitate this important fish food.

Up Wing Flies (e.g. Mayfly / Olives / March Brown)

The seasonal hatch of May Flies during late spring and early summer is a revered event that many river anglers. Sporting a distinctive upright wing the May Fly is just one of many species within the Latin order Ephemeroptera that is of interest to fly fishers. The diagram on page 41 details the lifecycle and see Stocking a River Fly Box on page 18 for the essential artificial flies required to imitate this important fish food.

Roof Wing Flies (e.g. Sandfly Sedge / Grannom / Silverhorns)

Flies that display wings with a roof like appearance while at rest are commonly referred to as Sedge or Caddis. These moth like insects have a haphazard approach to flying and can often be seen whirling in giddy formations close to the waters surface. Of particular importance to the fly angler choosing to fish a river, there are also plenty of situations when a still water angler will be relieved that they stocked a few Caddis imitations in their box! Flies with roof shaped wings are known as Trichoptera in Latin and follow the same lifecycle as flat wings, commencing their existence as an egg, prior to pupating and then emerging as an adult.

Hard Wing Flies (e.g. Yellow Sally, Needle Fly, Willow Fly)

A valuable addition to a Trout's diet and an anglers fly box within areas such as the North of England, in other regions the presence of Stoneflies is negligible to the point that they are not worth copying. Adult flies can be very large with a wing span of over 2 inches although the majority are much smaller. At rest the distinctly curved wings lie flat along the body and have a scaly appearance which makes this species simple to identify. Stoneflies spend much of their time as a nymph which crawls along the river or lake bed prior to hatching into an adult.

FISH FOOD

The Buzzer Lifecycle (Diptera / Chironomid)

Buzzer pupa are the bread and butter of a Trouts diet. Every angler should know about them! The fly begins life as a larva close to the lake/river bed, prior to pupating and making its way to the surface. At this point it is highly vunerable to attack, millions never make it to the surface! Those that do face a battle to break out of their pupal skin (shuck) prior to emerging as an adult. This stage of emergence is also an extremely vunerable time. These facts suggest that every angler should have a well stocked box of Buzzer pupa lifecycle imitations!

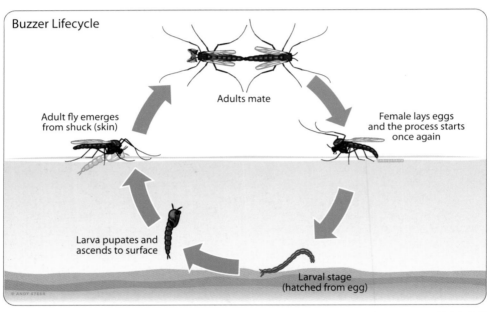

Buzzer Lifecycle

Adults mate

Adult fly emerges from shuck (skin)

Female lays eggs and the process starts once again

Larva pupates and ascends to surface

Larval stage (hatched from egg)

© ANDY STEER

A Bloodworm Imitation

An Adult Buzzer Imitation

Trout Bread and Butter - a Buzzer Pupa Imitation

The Upwing Lifecycle (Ephemeroptera)

Up wing flies are of particular importance to river anglers as they are consumed on a regular basis by the quarry. Fly boxes should be well stocked (see page 18/19) with representations to take advantage of this, mimicking the various stages of the lifecycle from nymph to adult. In particular take note of size, colouration and periods of the day in which certain species hatch. Turn over rocks to find nymphs in addition to maintaining constant observation for hatches and resulting fish activity. A well presented imitation of an Up wing fly often meets with a greedy reaction from a hungry Trout that are particularly predatory as the nymphs swim to the surface and hatch. Another important stage, often providing fantastic evening sport, is the period when Up wing flies give up the ghost and fall to the water as spent spinners. During this time Trout can become gluttonous, throwing caution to the wind and providing anglers with an opportunity not to be missed.

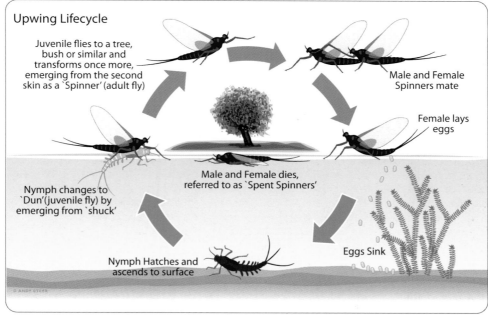

Upwing Lifecycle

Juvenile flies to a tree, bush or similar and transforms once more, emerging from the second skin as a `Spinner' (adult fly)

Male and Female Spinners mate

Female lays eggs

Nymph changes to `Dun'(juvenile fly) by emerging from `shuck'

Male and Female dies, referred to as `Spent Spinners'

Eggs Sink

Nymph Hatches and ascends to surface

An Up wing Nymph Imitation

An Adult Up wing Imitation

FLY FISHING TACTICS AND TECHNIQUE

Lake Fishing
Introduction

The secret to fly fishing success is to keep things simple, often following common sense and logical paths of thought to meet with the desired result. When first starting out go for the small stillwaters and then head to large venues. Confidence gained on the well stocked pools of a commercial fishery may seem a little artificial but provide a much needed training ground for novice anglers to cut their teeth and become confident with both tactics and technique. Visiting a large reservoir during these initial outings can be a daunting experience that may deter an angler from leaving the comfort of a small water for the rest of their days!

Lake fishing demands that an angler knows their territory, especially if the venue in question covers a large expanse. The easiest way to approach this situation is to slice the area up into individual sections, treating thousands of acres of water as small chunks of just few acres each. Look for bays, feeder streams and obvious features such as a hedgerow suddenly ceasing at the waters edge. Features such as these hold fish and should be ignored at an anglers peril! Depths can be guessed at by glancing towards the waters edge, a steep shoreline means that the water is highly likely to be deep, while a gently shelving bank results in shallow conditions.

Observation is one of the most important skills that a fly angler can develop. Be on the look out for birds such as Swallows feeding on insects, a sure sign that down below all sorts of bugs will be ascending to the surface or struggling to hatch, no doubt the fish will be there to take advantage! Take note of phenomena such as "slicks" or "wind lanes", areas of calm water that collect Trout food in abundance and provide success when elsewhere sport maybe slow. While casting, constantly scan the waters surface searching for clues to the fishes whereabouts. This may transpire as an obvious rise but with practice it is actually possible to recognise areas of nervous water created by a fish cruising near to the surface and displacing the surrounding liquid. Drop a fly near to the disturbance and quite often it will result in a take, very satisfying!

Never be afraid to ask fishery managers/owners for advice since for their business to succeed they will need your custom and that means they will be only too happy to advise on the best areas, tactics and technique. Likewise fellow fly fishers are often friendly folk who will in most circumstances divulge their successful line, retrieve and fly. Some may even hand over a sample of the deadly pattern! If possible join a fishing club to speed up the learning process and after each fishing session take time to make a note of temperatures, weather conditions, obvious hatches and try spooning fish captured to record feeding activity. In time each experience will build up into an indispensable pool of knowledge that can be used time and time again when at the waters edge. A fishing journal becomes an invaluable tool, tracing our progress through the years and collating many happy memories to be enjoyed by the fire on a cold winters evening.

Fishing tactics are an important consideration although quite often they need only be simple. Think of the venue in three dimensions, with varying depths which need to be covered thoroughly in order to locate the fish. In particular, observe the weather conditions and base tactics and line density around this. As a generalisation when the sun is up and the water temperature increases the fish will go deep, in cold weather they look for the warm layers deep down also. Anything in between is open for investigation and it is only the anglers willing to move, experiment with tactics, depth and retrieve that will gain regular success. Always try to "think like the fish" and consider their diet and habits when selecting tactics, it is a well used cliché but most certainly true! The following pages do not represent an exhaustive range of possibilities but merely tried and tested fishing methods that have stood the test of time. Finally, fly fishing is not an exact science and anglers never write the rule books, the fish do that! So when instinct suggests that a hunch may work, try it, there is nothing to lose and everything to gain. Good Fishing!

Where to Fish Lakes

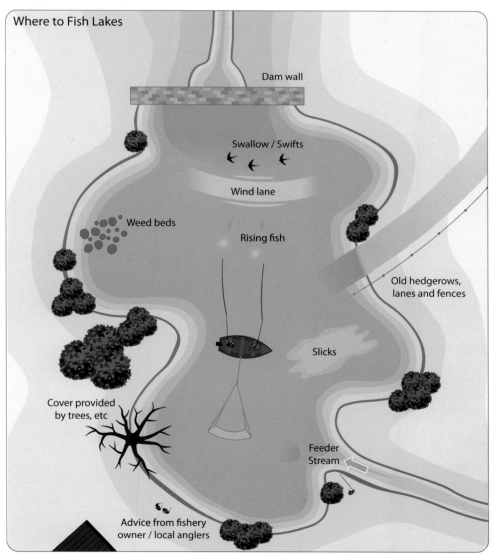

Dam wall

Swallow / Swifts

Wind lane

Weed beds

Rising fish

Old hedgerows, lanes and fences

Slicks

Cover provided by trees, etc

Feeder Stream

Advice from fishery owner / local anglers

Dry Fly

Wind

Dry Fly Fishing is pure pleasure and an extremely effective way of catching fish looking upwards for natural insects hatching or stranded on the waters surface. Cast a long leader with a single dry or possibly three as a team. An extremely good dry fly is the Hopper featured on page 15. Apply gink (floatant) to the fly sparingly and then look for rising fish, cast just in front of the rise as the fish move upwind. When a take transpires, in the form of a fish showing its head, LIFT!

Swinging buzzers on the wind

Cross Wind

Buzzers are taken by Trout on a regular basis, so fishing with their imitations is a highly successful tactic. Cast across the wind and allow the artificial pattern to swing with the current, providing it with a very natural drift. Keep in touch with the line by maintaining a very slow retrieve. Takes can be gentle, transpiring as a heavy feeling on the line, or incredible arm wrenching pulls! Use heavy buzzers to gain more depth.

Figure of eight

Figure of Eight fishing is popular with many anglers. It is a style of retrieve used to either just keep in touch with the line or fish the artificial back in a slow fashion. Use a faster retrieve to give the fly a jerky movement and go slower to allow the fly to drift with the wind. To figure of 8 retrieve: 1) Take the line between thumb and first finger of the line controlling hand 2) Make a short pull of 2 inches 3) Rotate the remaining three fingers over the top of this section of line and pull 4) Repeat from step 1

New Zealand Dropper

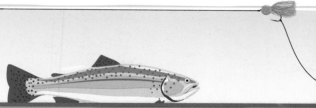

New Zealand Dropper fishing has gained in popularity over the years, first starting with dry flies used as an indicator, before the advent of bungs, a highly buoyant and visible marker many made from plastazote (ethafoam) or similar man made material. Blood knot a length of leader to the bend of a dry fly or bung, the length can be varied according to the depth required. Tie on a fly such as a Black or Olive Buzzer to this section of leader, cast out and then watch the indicator. If it disappears, Lift! A great way of presenting buzzers in their natural state as they drift upon the wind, also a great method for finding fish holding depth.

A team of flies

A Team of Flies can be fished on a variety of lines. A heavy fly can be fished on the point (furthest fly from the fly line) for example, to pull one or two others deep. Another use of a team is to fish a highly visible lure on the top dropper to attract fish, often they will follow this and then turn on more imitative patterns fished on the middle dropper and point.

Lure stripping

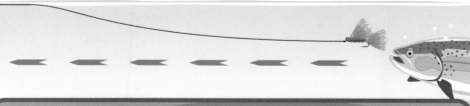

Lure Stripping, is exactly that! Throw out a lure on its own, or as part of team and then pull back at high speed. Perhaps not the most interesting fishing, but at times highly effective, especially if fish are not willing to take imitative patterns. Lures often work well during early season and on newly introduced fish. Floating, intermediate and sinking lines are all worth a try. Favourite colours include Black, Orange and White.

Stop start retrieve

Stop & Start retrieving is a great way to fool the fish and relevant for a variety of lines, flies and conditions. Twitch the fly back with small, sharp jerks. Then stop. Then start again! Takes often come just as the fly begins to move or just as it stops and drops through the water layer. Very effective when fishing Damsel nymphs or teams of flies with a lure as an attractor. Vary the retrieve as much as possible until something provides success.

Washing line

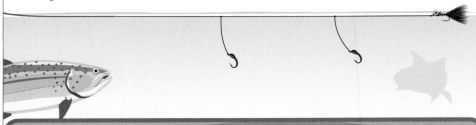

The Washing Line is another fairly modern technique. Tie a buoyant fly on to the point of a leader and then add a couple of Buzzers, Diawl Bachs or similar to the droppers. Cast out using a variety of lines and fish slowly. Every now and again suddenly speed the retrieve up and then stop, the buoyant fly will begin to rise, producing a very natural effect on the flies in the team, often resulting in confident takes. Another go anywhere tactic that works on a regular basis!

Booby fishing

Lake Bed

Booby fishing is excellent during early season or bright sun light when the fish go deep. Short and long leaders work fished on very fast sinking lines. Once the fly is deep, it will pop up off the bottom or sit mid water. An ultra slow retrieve often results in taps, allow a couple and then STRIKE! Another proven method is to give the line several sharp pulls and then stop, wait for a take immediately afterwards. Beware, this tactic should not be used for catch and release fishing.

Flies or Tactics?

Fishing tactics are very often far more important than the fly pattern. Hours spent pouring over the fly box wastes valuable fishing time and there are rarely any magical patterns that result in instant success! Instead think far more about the depth that a fly is being fished and the speed of retrieve. For example, many anglers throw out a floating line and then pull the fly straight back in! This means that the fly will only ever fish just sub surface. Experiment by casting and then counting the fly down for 10 seconds, try this for 15 minutes and then change to 15 seconds down. This approach often results in success as an angler will find the correct holding depth of the fish by trial and error. As confidence grows, conditions can be noted and quick tactical changes made accordingly. Remember the much used saying "your fly can't catch a fish while it is out of the water!" Above all be observant of weather conditions, birds feeding and natural insects/flies stranded in the water, all provide vital clues that can lead to a rewarding day. Tightlines!

Sinking Fly Lines

Many individuals entering into the world of fly fishing assume that casts are made to simulate natural insects dancing upon the waters surface. This is certainly true of traditional techniques such as "dapping", but in reality contemporary tactics extend much further than this.

Trout can often be found feeding several feet below the surface on a varied diet including aquatic insects/beetles, pupa, larvae and even small fish. In these circumstances an angler must follow the fish and present artificials at the correct depth, in fact, this is perhaps one of the most important considerations when choosing tactics and technique. Get the depth right, followed by speed of retrieve and fly choice can become almost insignificant!

Modern day fly fishing has evolved into a myriad of different fly lines boasting non stretch cores, super smooth coatings and various other manufacturing claims all designed to lure anglers themselves into a purchase. However, the most important development is the wide ranging depths that some of these new lines can achieve. All newcomers to the sport should cast with a floating line only in the first instance, until the technique is well practiced and consistent. Following this achievement the first line to add to the tackle bag is a slow sinker, referred to as an intermediate. There are many on the market but look for something that sinks at around 2" per second, the packaging will provide details. Intermediates are ideal for fishing just below the surface when pulled fast or allow to sink for an extended period to fish mid water. If more depth is required, then a fast sinker would be a wise choice with a sink rate of 3"/4" per second.

The benefit of collecting several different sink rates of fly lines over the years is the anglers ability to remain consistently within the quarries realm. Floating lines coupled with long leaders and heavy flies will achieve depth, but as the line is retrieved the flies will rise steadily, remaining in the taking area for just a short length of time. A sinking line will fish through this taking area for longer, prior to rising to the surface, see diagram on page 48 for a sinking fly line guide. It is also worth noting that most sinking lines come in a wide range of colours (see photo on page 48), starting with light greens and blues or even clear for intermediates. Fast sinking lines are often dark green or brown, while super fast sinkers come in very dark brown or even black. This knowledge is important when out fishing, if you see a fellow angler enjoying success, note the fly line colour they are using, it could be a vital clue!

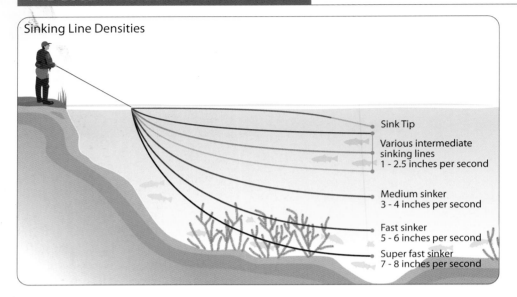

Sinking Line Densities

Sink Tip

Various intermediate
sinking lines
1 - 2.5 inches per second

Medium sinker
3 - 4 inches per second

Fast sinker
5 - 6 inches per second

Super fast sinker
7 - 8 inches per second

How to use a Sinking Line.

Cast out and as the line hits the water, give 2 long pulls of around one foot, to straighten the line and leader. Then begin counting based on the depth being fished. Try 10 seconds for a quarter of an hour, then 15 seconds for a further 15 minutes. Maintain steady contact with the line using a very slow figure 8 retrieve, even while sinking, as fish often take the fly as it descends, referred to as a "drop take". Continue to wait for longer periods of time until eventually the taking depth is found. In cold weather the fish are likely to head for deep water and warm layers known as thermoclines. In these circumstances start by fishing deep, counting down for long periods e.g. 35 seconds, until the leader snags the bottom. Then, on the next cast count to 30 in the certain knowledge that the fly is not far from the lake bed. Continue counting up, 25, 20, 15 etc., until once again the fish holding depth is found. This technique is also worth trying in very hot conditions when the Trout are seeking cooler water. If fishing alongside an angling partner, try different lines between you as this can help

locate the fish quickly. Finally, when completing all retrieves with a sinking line, pull the line steadily towards the surface with the rod tip and pause briefly. Hanging the flies momentarily in this manner can be deadly. Prior to recasting, use a roll cast to bring the flies fully to the surface and then commence the overhead once again. This is an extremely important safety measure, NEVER attempt to cast a sinking line without rolling it to the surface!

FLY FISHING TACTICS AND TECHNIQUE
River Fishing
Introduction

Rivers are wonderful places to enjoy quality time fishing and are nowhere near so expensive as many people assume. Chalkstreams in the South of England certainly do not fall within this category, but if an angler can endure losing a few flies in un-manicured bank side vegetation while capturing fish of perhaps just a few inches, then there are a huge range of value for money options available. Schemes such as the West Country Angling Passport (see page 58) provide the public with access to miles of superb fishing in unspoilt surroundings with just the odd Otter, Kingfisher or Dipper for company and all for just a few pounds. In fact this is what River fishing is all about; no crowds, just the therapeutic sound of trickling water in the background and Kingfishers for company. What better way to enjoy a day away from the office, the stresses and strains of every day life? Leaving the poetic descriptions behind for a moment, the serenity can degenerate into a stream of bad language and frustration if a few general rules are not observed when casting over running water!

Fish inhabiting river venues across the U.K. are often wild, fending for themselves and certainly not brought up on a meal or two of pellets each day. Instead their existence depends entirely on cunning and instinctive, split second reactions. A Trout caught out snoozing might become a predators dinner while a lack of observance may leave its own meal to go begging. An angler approaching their quarry with this knowledge has an advantage because they are likely to stay low, cast with care and disturb the target as little as possible. In particular remember that Trout have a design fault, a blind zone to the rear (see page 37) that renders them unaware of an anglers presence, so where possible sneak up behind the fish to a position as near to the subject as possible. This allows for simple presentation, less drag and effective hook ups. The angler who gains a close proximity to their quarry should observe carefully, paying particular attention to the depth, natural insects being consumed and any particular habits the fish may display, such as taking every 3rd fly or cruising to a certain point to intercept a morsel of food.

Above all, remember to think like the fish and constantly be on the look out for their basic requirements of FOOD, SHELTER & OXYGEN. Treat walking along a stretch of river (referred to as a beat) as a natural history experience, observing where each Trout is stationed (Polaroid sunglasses are a must!) and it will soon be realised that each individual is positioned to gain maximum benefit from their situation. Trout require a steady flow of oxygen over their gills and will do as little as possible to earn their subsistence. They also need the safety of a subsurface bolt hole for quick evacuation should they feel threatened. Use this information wisely and the ability to "read the river" will soon transpire; watercraft is an invaluable tool that will result in many contented hours of extremely satisfying sport.

Approach a river for the first time after considerable casting practice as competent casting displaying tight, accurate loops will provide an angler with an array of opportunities not available to those individuals who ignore the fact that this skill is the glue that holds everything together. Finally, wild fish are a valuable commodity that demand a conservation minded attitude. If fish are sought for the table there are plenty of well stocked small stillwaters that can add to the contents of the freezer, a wild fish caught and released will be a little wiser for their efforts and lives to fight another day. The following sections detail likely Trout habitat and a few proven methods that should help winkle out a fish or two. Tightlines!

Where to Fish Rivers

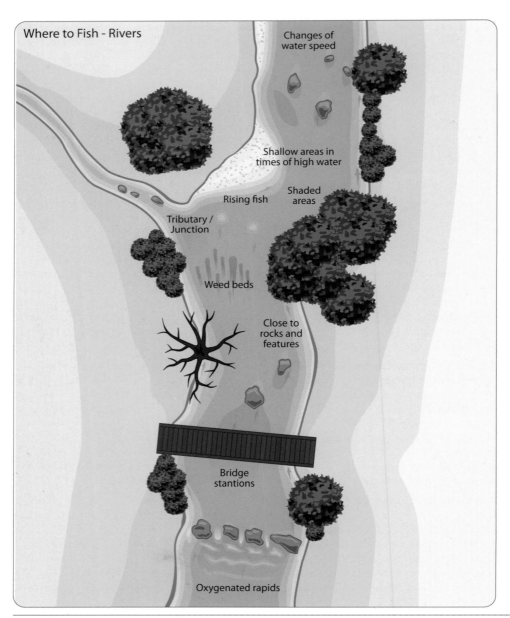

Where to Fish - Rivers

Changes of water speed

Shallow areas in times of high water

Rising fish

Shaded areas

Tributary / Junction

Weed beds

Close to rocks and features

Bridge stantions

Oxygenated rapids

Dry Fly

Dry Fly is one of the most favoured of river fishing tactics. Look for a rising Trout or cast to areas likely to hold fish. Approach the fish from behind, remembering that they have excellent forward and side vision but little behind them (see page 37) Check if there is any hatch about and study carefully what (if any) naturals the fish are taking. Catch a few and pick out a likely looking artificial dry fly, paying particular attention to size and colour. Tie this to a Knotless Tapered Leader (see page 10), apply floatant (Gink) to the fly. Make a careful cast ensuring that the fly line lands behind the fish, the leader crossing above and the fly several feet upstream. Eliminate as much drag as possible from the line, so that the fly travels downstream, back towards the angler/fish, with a natural LIFT!

New Zealand Dropper

New Zealand Dropper is an excellent river fishing tactic and provides the angler with 2 chances, presenting artificial patterns both surface and subsurface. Tie on a tapered leader and add a dry fly such as an Adams or Elk Hair Sedge (see page 19). Tie a length of leader suitable for the depth to be fished to the bend of the dry fly hook and based on the assumed feeding position of the Trout/Grayling. Tie a nymph to this second section of leader, such as a Copper John (see page 18) or Pheasant Tail Nymph. Cast upstream, to an area well above the anticipated fish position, allowing enough time for the nymph to sink. Watch the dry fly carefully, if it disappears, LIFT! Be on the look out for fish taking the Dry Fly and check local rules as some rivers do not allow this technique. For wild rivers, with fast runs, deep pots and similar fish holding features, this is a deadly tactic, especially when the fish are not rising regularly. Again this rig should be fished upstream and attention should be centred on reducing drag.

Spider Fishing

Shallow Water

Water Flow

River Bed

Spiders, do not in fact imitate the eight legged creepy crawly but instead hatching, dead or drowning flies being washed downstream by the force of the current. Fishing spider patterns (see page 18) over shallow water is particularly productive. Cast downstream at a 45 degree angle and allow the current to swing the flies across river, takes can be savage and often the fish will hook themselves. Experiment by mending the line to reduce drag, see page 54. Mending the line will allow the flies to fish deeper and slower, providing the fish with the chance to see the fly. Figure Eight retrieving as the fly crosses the water also works. Look for streamy areas of water, often referred to as a riffle, this is an ideal location for trying out spider patterns. Some very skilled anglers fish spider patterns upstream with great success and this is certainly a highly effective technique to be pursued once a good foundation of basic techniques have been practiced.

An angler tries his luck with a czech nymph

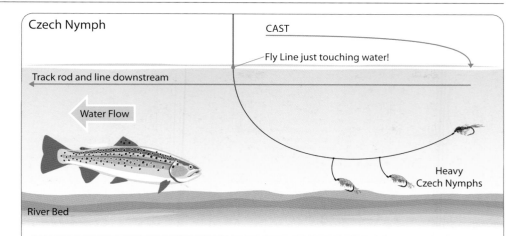

Czech Nymph

CAST

Fly Line just touching water!

Track rod and line downstream

Water Flow

Heavy Czech Nymphs

River Bed

Czech Nymph Style / Bugging is particularly effective in fast flowing areas of a river and over both deep and shallow water. This technique can be devastating, but only if extreme care is taken to control the fly line, leader and ultimately the flies. Begin by constructing a leader suitable for the depth to be fished. Czech Nymph leaders are usually shorter than those used for other techniques, at 4 to 6 ft long. Tie in one or two droppers and attach heavy flies, such as Czech style nymphs (see page 18) or similar patterns with some kind of additional weight, for example, a gold head. Tie a smaller, light weight fly to the point. Casts are more a lob upstream, directly above the angler, do not attempt to cast conventionally as this can result in horrendous tangles! When the flies strike the water and begin to sink, raise the rod high, allowing only the very tip of the fly line to touch the waters surface. Try and keep the rod directly above the flies, allowing a vertical presentation and track the tip carefully downstream following the artificials journey. As the flies pass, begin dropping the rod steadily towards the waters surface, raise and then repeat. Work backwards and forwards across sections of rivers, trying to present the flies at as many angles as possible. Takes come in various forms including a twitch of the fly line, the line sliding away or simply stopping for no apparent reason. Even the merest hint of a take should be met with a firm lift! This technique requires many years of practice to become accomplished and some anglers don't consider this to be true fly fishing, however, it is a highly skilled technique that can take fish in the very worst conditions when other tactics would fail. A long rod of 9' to 10' for a #4 or #5 line is advised for those anglers who regularly use this method.

A Czech Nymph

A Copper John

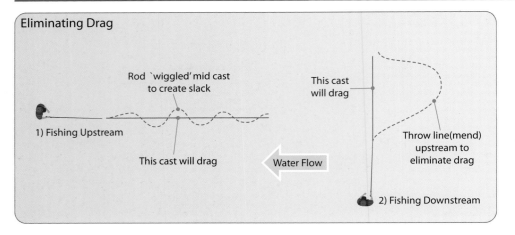

Eliminating Drag

Rod `wiggled' mid cast to create slack

This cast will drag

1) Fishing Upstream

This cast will drag

Water Flow

Throw line(mend) upstream to eliminate drag

2) Fishing Downstream

When a natural fly hatches or becomes trapped within the surface tension, it floats naturally along with the current, very often right into the mouth of a waiting fish! Fly anglers must copy this process by making a cast and then providing sufficient slack within the line to slow the fly down or in the case of nymph fishing, gain the artificial a little more depth and valuable extra seconds within the Trout/Graylings domain. Dry flies must appear to fish naturally in time with current, flowing to the fish at the same speed and in the same direction. If a tell tale "V wake" appears behind the artificial fly, it is now "dragging" and will appear incorrectly to the fish. In many cases it will be totally ignored and if unlucky, it could spook a fish to the point that it no longer feeds until it feels safe once more. Drag is a real problem for river fly anglers and can be the difference between success and failure, so learning the skills required to eliminate this problem is time very well spent. The diagram above provides a basic overview of methods used to eliminate drag.

The angler in position 1 is casting upstream with a dry fly. If the line remains straight it will pull the leader quickly causing the dry fly to drag. By making a small wiggle of the rod, mid cast, as the line straightens out, slack will be placed within the line. This provides the angler with valuable seconds as the current takes a few moments to remove the slack, leaving the artificial to float gracefully downstream in a natural manner. There are many casts available to produce slack line and a drag free drift including the wiggle cast, pile cast or aerial mend.

The angler in position 2 is fishing spiders across the downstream current, which is causing the patterns to traverse too quickly across the river and without sufficient depth. By throwing slack line upstream, while feeding a little line, the fly is allowed to achieve a greater depth while also slowing down. This process is called "mending" and can be repeated several times within one drift if necessary. Experiment with different mend sizes and feeding extra line to obtain a variety of depths and speeds.

FLY FISHING TACTICS AND TECHNIQUE

How to Play, Land and Release Trout

Imagine standing next to a favourite venue, the birds singing, a warm breeze blowing and here and there the gentle "sip" of a Trout. The line is steadily being retrieved, imparting an enticing action into the artificial and creating the illusion of life. Then, suddenly the line tenses momentarily, the trigger for an angler to concentrate fully, blocking out all other distractions. There it is again, a definite pressure felt over the finger tip gently trapping the line against the rod blank. Speed up the retrieve and bingo, this time the line snaps tight and a fish is on! This is what fly fishing is all about, but it so often ends in tears, especially for novice fly anglers. In a fit of excitement all knowledge is thrown out of the window as the angler desperately attempts to winch the angry fish towards land, with a loud "ping" the leader pops leaving a Trout with an unwanted item of jewellery and the angler with a heavy heart! Follow this simple procedure and a more favourable outcome should transpire.

1) As soon as the fish is felt, raise the rod high. Use the clock and think 11 o'clock for a right handed caster and 1 o'clock for a left hander. This will ensure that the rod acts as a shock absorber and protects the leader.

2) After the initial hook up the fish will often realise its mistake and make a strong run. At this point use the first finger of the rod hand (trapping the fly line), as a brake. Imagine coming down a hill using the brakes, and gently ease the pressure off the line allowing the fish to swim away, or "run".

3) As soon as the fish halts, put the brakes back on and pull line in as quickly as possible, be wary that the fish may take off once more. If it does so, ease off with the braking finger and allow it take as much line as required.

4) If the fish heads towards a snag, apply pressure with the rod in the opposite direction. This is called "side strain".

5) Once the fish is beaten, lying on its side and calm, place the landing net deep below the surface and pull the fish steadily over the top. Be aware that this is often the most important stage of the fight and the most likely point that a loss will be endured. If the fish makes another run, once again, ease off the brakes!

6) Congratulations, a fish in the net! Either dispatch with the priest immediately while the fish is still in the net, or if the fish is to be released, keep it in the water. Remove the hook, gently support and release.

equipment and licences

The Essential Selection Equipment & Safety

Introduction: Sadly every year anglers receive serious injury or are even killed while out fishing. Common sense often saves the day, but here are a few basic guidelines to adhere to while out fishing. Don't let your fishing trip end in tragedy.

essential safety

Polarised Sunglasses / Eye Protection: Every year fly anglers are seriously injured by hooks striking them in the eye. To paint a chilling picture, imagine for just one moment what it would be like to have a piece of extremely sharp metal hit you in the eye at considerable speed? The result will be reduced sight at best, the reality is the possibility of becoming blind. It is very rare for the fly to come anywhere near the face, especially when the cast is practiced to a high standard, so do not be put off by this statement. Even so, accidents happen, so please ... ALWAYS WEAR EYE PROTECTION. There are no second chances.

With the safety aspect covered it is also worth noting sunglasses as an important fishing tool. A polarised lens will cut out glare on the waters surface, therefore assisting with the task of spotting fish. Particularly helpful when stalking or fishing for species situated in broken water found on rivers. One well known New Zealand guide was heard to say that he would "rather leave home without his fly boxes than his polarised sunglasses!"

Hat / Cap / Head Protection: Next on the list of important safety items is head protection. Again it is rare for the fly to strike an angler if the casting technique is good. However, a cap or hat of some description guards against injury. Caps are also excellent at reducing glare from the sun which assists fish spotting while helping to maintain body heat, a great deal of which can be lost via the head.

General Safety: It is well worth informing someone of location details if fishing a particularly far off or treacherous venue. A mobile phone is an excellent source of communication for example and can be kept safe in a water proof pouch such as an "Aquapac". Look out for overhead power cables, carbon fibre rods are superb conductors of electricity and should be avoided at all times. Electricity can jump from a cable to a rod, so never believe that you actually have to touch the line to receive injury! A wading staff or stick is superb on a river or in deep water to assist balance. Some anglers may also wish to wear a buoyancy aid or lifejacket, especially when fishing from boats or in a river. Being able to swim is of course a great asset but do not rely on this alone, even the strongest of swimmers are helpless if they have banged their head upon entrance to the water, while clothing becomes heavy once immersed, sapping the energy from even the fittest people. We are increasingly reminded of the risks of skin cancer caused by too much sun. The water reflects the suns rays back into an anglers face, so always cover up with a high factor sun block or similar protection. Finally, carry plenty of spare food, water and clothing, while a basic medical kit may seem over the top but could prove its worth in the event of an emergency.

ESSENTIAL CLOTHING

There is nothing worse than a fishing session spent enduring rain dripping down the neck. Cold soon sets in and before long the enjoyment will be lost, the whole reason we go fishing in the first place! Clothing for serious anglers should include a good quality jacket, preferably made of Gortex or a similar product and with a wind proof lining. Cheap products without this important feature are available, but it will seem like false economy when a cold wind whips up! Good waterproof trousers are also a must have, a jacket is no good if the water drops on to exposed legs clad in highly absorbent jeans or similar. This garment is also ideal for sessions in muddy conditions, saving everyday clothing underneath from becoming spoiled. Gloves, scarves, good quality fleeces, socks and hats are all well worth packing, after all it is far better to wear too much clothing and be able to take it off. A spare set of garments is also recommended just in case an unexpected dunking is sustained!

ESSENTIAL TACKLE

Introduction: The basic tackle requirements are covered at the beginning of this book (Page 6 to 9), however there are a few other accessories and important pieces of equipment that an angler should carry to ensure a successful day. Where possible try to pack light, as mobility is one factor that makes fly fishing all the more appealing. Here is a short guide to the most essential items.

Rod: Seems obvious, but remember to pick it up! More than one angler has arrived at their destination only to realise that they didn't pack a rod in the car! For stillwater Trout Fishing a rod of 9' 6" rated for a 7 line is perfect while most small rivers can be tackled with an 8' #4. Refer to page 6 for further details regarding choosing a suitable rod for your chosen venue. It is also worth considering purchasing 2 rods, just in case one breaks while out fishing!

Reel: Trout fishing in the U.K. does not demand a high quality reel or drag system, although a good quality reel could be classed as an item of jewellery, finishing off a rod perfectly! This is purely down to personal preference. However, if fishing for hard fighting species such as Salmon or Sea Trout, more consideration should be paid to the strength of the drag and if fly fishing in saltwater, look for a non-corrosive reel. Large Arbours are in vogue and do have many advantages, such as storing the line in neat open coils. Ensure that your reel is loaded with ample backing prior to winding on the fly line.

Fly Line: A Floating line is a must have. Reservoir anglers will also require a variety of sinking lines. Purchase good quality fly lines that have a smooth surface and therefore assist casting. In the main go for the very effective Weight Forward (WF) profile and ensure that the line has been matched to the rod. Clean floating lines frequently with one of the cleaners widely available. **Note: DO NOT** clean sinking lines with commercially available cleaning products, it will make the line float! Instead use water with a **very small** amount of detergent. Cleaned regularly a line should last at least two seasons.

LICENCES AND PERMITS

Rod Licence: When fishing in England & Wales an Environment Agency rod licence will be required, available from post offices and via www.environment-agency.gov.uk or telephone 0844 800 5386. There are various categories available for either Trout & Non Migratory Fish (Coarse fish such as Carp for example) or for Migratory Fish such as Salmon or Sea Trout. Prices alter depending on the licence required. Concessions for O.A.Ps and Children are available.

Permits: A licence does not give an angler the right to fish! Always check to see if your venue requires a separate permit. There are many small waters and reservoirs offering their services and widely advertised. It is actually a misconception that rivers are hard to access. Try local tourist offices, check the classifieds in angling magazines or research on the web. Various schemes are available up and down the country providing budget priced river fishing, details follow:

West Country Angling Passport – www.angling2000.org.uk **Tel: 01579 372140**
Wye & Usk Passport - www.wyeuskfoundation.org **Tel: 01982 551520**
Go Wild in Eden - www.go-wild.org.uk **Tel: 01768 866788**
Tyne Angling Passport - www.tyneriverstrust.org

ESSENTIAL TACKLE ACCESSORIES

Waistcoat or Pack: Store all your gear neatly and close to hand (see diagram right).

Leaders: Carry a variety of Knotless Tapered Leaders and spools of line. See pages 10 and 11 for more information on how to construct a leader. Co polymer and Fluorocarbon leader will be required depending on water conditions and fishing tactics.

Nips: Hang them on some kind of retractor to keep close at hand, perfect for snipping leader quickly and saves the dentist bill!

Flies: One of the least expensive items and yet, perhaps the most important! A good stock of Wets, Dries, Nymphs and Lures is required. See pages 13 to 19 for information on how to stock a fly box and pages 38 to 41 for a guide to identifying the various natural diet available.

Floatant / Sinkant: Use floatant to keep dry flies buoyant. Floatant can also be used to treat the front of a floating line if it is sinking. Sinkant is used on the leader to remove grease, helping it to sink and therefore making it less obvious to the fish. Sinkant also removes the shine from a leader, although it is not required when using fluorocarbon leader material. Sinkant is particularly important when dry fly fishing.

Net: Assists landing a fish, especially a large specimen. Many nets are available on the market, pick something suitable for the chosen venue and ensure that the net is made from knotless mesh. Knotted mesh is now illegal!

Forceps: Great for flattening barbs on hooks and for removing flies from fish.

Priest: Carry this to dispatch fish quickly and humanely.

Bass Bag: Moisten with water and leave in the shade to maintain freshness of the catch. Never use plastic carrier bags or leave the catch at the side of the venue. This can actually partially cook the fish!

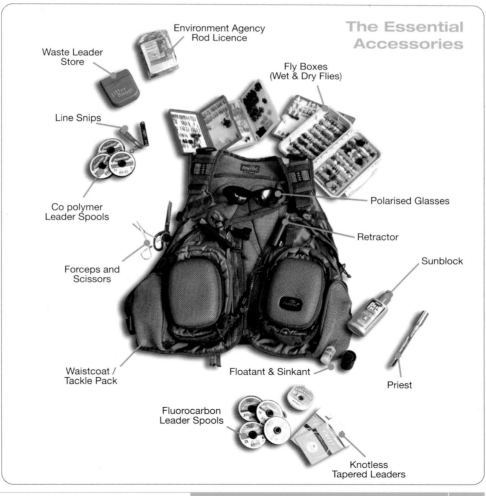

The Essential Accessories

Environment Agency Rod Licence

Waste Leader Store

Fly Boxes (Wet & Dry Flies)

Line Snips

Co polymer Leader Spools

Polarised Glasses

Retractor

Sunblock

Forceps and Scissors

Waistcoat / Tackle Pack

Floatant & Sinkant

Priest

Fluorocarbon Leader Spools

Knotless Tapered Leaders

GLOSSARY

A

AFTM – Association of Fishing Tackle Manufacturers, designates line and rod ratings.
ARBOUR – The central area of a fly reel.

B

BACKING – Thin line wound on before fly line to increase spool diameter and reduce line memory.
BELLY – Section of a fly line carrying the most weight.
BLANK – Tubular sections of a fly rod to which rings are bound to enable the passage of a fly line.
BUNG – Buoyant fly used as an indicator.

C

CAST – Physical act of presenting an artificial bait/fly to a fish using rod and line.
COPOLYMER – A popular low diameter leader material.

D

D LOOP – Term used to describe the shape of line hanging behind the rod prior to the forward stroke of a roll cast.
DENSITY – The sink rate of a fly line.
DOUBLE HAUL – Casting technique used to increase load upon the rod and generate high line speeds.
DOUBLE TAPER (DT) – A fly line that tapers at both ends.
DRAG – Unnatural presentation of an artificial fly, causing it to move faster than the speed of the current.
DRAG SYSTEM – Metal disc or similar located inside a fly reel. Operated by a knob usually located on the rear of the reel body and used to apply/release pressure on the spool.
DROPPER – The spare end (tag) of a knot used to join 2 pieces of line together to which further flies can be tied.
DRY FLY – An artificial pattern that sits on or just in the surface film.

E

EMERGER – A natural fly about to break out of its SHUCK.

F

FALSE CAST – Mid air movement of a fly line completed without touching the water.
FEATURES – Areas that provide fish habitat, such as feeder streams, submerged river beds and drop offs.
FLOATANT – Gel or wax like substance applied to dry flies to assist buoyancy.
FLUOROCARBON – A modern leader material with a low refractive index, widely acclaimed to be more successful than normal nylon/copolymers in certain conditions.

H

HACKLE – Feather wound at the eye of a dry fly to create a bushy appearance and assist buoyancy. Also wound through bodies and positioned at the collar of various wet fly patterns to generate disturbance or simulate features of a natural insect.
HATCH – The moment when natural flies take to the wing, large groups emerging in this way often trigger a rise.
HEAD SECTION – Another term used to describe the section of a fly line with the largest diameter and carrying the most weight. See BELLY.

L

LARVA – First stage of certain species of natural fly, after the egg. Similar to a worm in appearance. Caddis larva and Bloodworm are good examples.
LEADER – Section of copolymer, fluorocarbon etc., attached to the front section of a fly line, providing a nearly invisible link to the artificial patterns.
LEADER SINK – Putty like substance designed to remove grease/shine from the leader and help it sink.
LOADING – A rod flexing due to tension created by the weight of a fly line during a casting stroke.
LOOP – The shape of a fly line as it unrolls on the forward and back casts.
LURES – Artificial fly patterns designed to motivate aggression within fish, rather than copy their natural diet.

M

MARROW SPOON – A tool used to examine the stomach contents of captured fish.

MEND – Applying slack to a fly line to reduce the effects of a current on the line and designed to reduce the problem of DRAG.

MONOFILAMENT – Widely used variety of leader material.

N

NYMPH – Sub surface insect that lives its life under rocks and in weeds, prior to hatching out into a fly. Preyed upon by Trout and Grayling.

P

PARACHUTES – Style of artificial fly incorporating a horizontal hackle wound around a wing post that ensures all fibres touch the waters surface. Gaining in popularity over traditional collar hackled patterns.

POINT FLY – The last fly fished in a team, furthest from the fly line.

PRIEST – Heavy metal or wooden object used to humanely dispatch Trout.

PUPA – The point in the lifecycle of flat and roof wing flies when the insect metamorphoses from a larva into a fly covered in a thin skin that is used to ascend to the surface of a lake/river.

R

REEL FOOT – Section of a reel used to attach to a fly rod.

RETRIEVE – Pulling fly line back in after a cast to animate an artificial fly or take up slack depending on venue, tactics and technique.

RIFFLE – Area of shallow, fast flowing water with a high oxygen content found at the tail of a pool.

RISE – The moment when a fish breaks the waters surface to intercept a natural insect.

RUNNING LINE – Low diameter section of a fly line, positioned behind the HEAD or BELLY of a weight forward fly line/shooting head and designed to reduce drag within the rods rings during the final SHOOT.

S

SEAM – Where fast and slow moving water meet on a river creating an invisible barrier that traps food channelling it to the fish and consequently a highly productive area that should be cast to regularly.

SHOOT – The moment when line is released during FALSE CASTING.

SHUCK – Left over skin used by a natural fly to ascend to the lake/river surface. Often consumed by Trout/Grayling.

SINKANT – See LEADER SINK.

SLICKS – Narrow areas of calm water with an oily appearance that trap food on lakes and attract Trout.

SPEYS – Style of roll casting often incorporating a large change of direction and useful in enclosed conditions.

SPOOL – The part of a reel used to store a fly line.

STICK – Tension on a fly line created by water, also referred to as an "anchor point". A small amount of stick can be beneficial when applied to certain casts, too much can ruin the outcome.

T

TAG END – Spare/loose end of a knot, sometimes used as a DROPPER.

TAPER – Section of fly line or leader gradually decreasing in diameter.

THERMOCLINES – Layers of warm and cold water.

TIPPET – Sometimes used instead of the term LEADER but more useful as a description of an additional section of line knotted to the end of a leader.

TURN OVER – The moment when a LOOP fully extends, hopefully presenting the artificial flies as far away from the fly line as possible.

W

WATERCRAFT – The ability to evaluate a venue and make informed choices of technique, tactics and equipment/flies based on observation and experience.

WEIGHT FORWARD (WF) – A fly line with the majority of the weight positioned at the front.

WET FLY – An artificial fly designed to be fished subsurface.

WIND LANE – Similar to a SLICK but larger.

WRIST BREAK – The action of a wrist pivoting in an uncontrolled manner during a cast. The cardinal casting sin leading to low back casts, wide loops and inefficient presentation!

INDEX

ACKNOWLEDGEMENTS

My first casts were attempted under the watchful eye of a local postman in my hometown of Exford in Somerset. Colin spent time teaching me to cast and tie flies which triggered the passion that has lead to the career I enjoy today. I met Colin recently for the first time in years and look forward to casting a line with him once again in the future.

Dad is not here anymore and unfortunately never lived to find out that I do now make a living from fishing! Dad was more interested in my school work for obvious reasons, but it was he who got me out fishing for the very first time and fired my enthusiasm. Sadly Mum is no longer with us either, but she provided plenty of support to a teenager with a dream. That dream became reality through one of the most highly respected instructors in the world, Simon Gawesworth. Simon took me under his wing and taught me many of the teaching methods and practices that I still pass on today.

Henry Gilbeys passion for fishing is infectious and it shows within his photography which appears throughout the book. These images and the text were originally put together by Lou Boniface under much pressure and more recently her husband Mike Boniface co-ordinated the 2nd edition designed by Guy Rayment. The brand new diagrams are the genius work of Andy Steer located in the Netherlands.

There are tons of other people that I should mention but could not possibly write these acknowledgements without mentioning Alasdare Lambert. Al has helped Hart Flyshop to become the success it is today through many hours of careful tutoring via business coaching company Shirlaws. Jon Hettle has also been a primary source of advice and inspiration, if only he would get out of the office and go fishing more! To this list I should add names such as Alex Bobba, Russell Hill, Paul Arden, Michael Evans, William Daniel, Karl King, Iain Barr, James Warbrick-Smith, Andrew Hedger and Lee Sennington, there are many more and I apologise profusely if I have missed you!

Finally since originally writing and publishing this book back in 2006 I have become the proud father of two awesome children. My little boy Chester is already well into fishing at age 2 ½ and Scarlett age 1 ½ is definitely looking interested from the sidelines. They are brilliant and actually a great way to wind down after a hard day at the waters edge! Of course I have the easy bit; it is my wife Sue, full time Mum and director within Hart Flyshop that does the real work! Thank you for all you do, the children and I know how lucky we are.